Ilene Nathanson

CAREGIVING CONFIDENTIAL:

Path of Meaning

CAREGIVING CONFIDENTIAL: Path of Meaning

© 2022 Ilene Nathanson

Paperback ISBN: 978-1-66784-521-0

eBook ISBN: 978-1-66784-522-7

To my mother, Helen Ann Weinrib Nathanson, who does "not go gently into the night"; but rather inspires those around her with her dignity, courage and passion for living.

To all of the caregivers, whom I have met on this path of meaning, who have invested their lives in the support of those in their care.

CONTENTS

PREFACE

Caregiving for aging spouses and parents is a minefield of explosive problems. There are numerous books about how to navigate the medical and governmental complexes that are involved with aging. Awareness of the heavy mental and physical burdens that are often placed on caregivers has been growing. Self-help books abound, but sometimes what a caregiver needs is simply to find solace in a friend, even better a friend who has been through a caregiver situation.

The inspiration for this book came exactly from the author's having had the experience of finding solace in friends, listening to their stories, sharing stories with them, groaning at the tales of irrational and angry behavior, guffawing at the tales of situations and actions so ridiculously wild and funny that no one thought anyone would or could ever believe them.

Dr. Nathanson is a clinical social worker and a retired university professor who has taught courses and written articles and books on aging and gerontology; however, this book is NOT intended to be an academic treatise on aging. Her background will lend knowledgeable oversight to the content and contain many of her own experiences caring for a parent. Her stories and that knowledge will be integrated into those of friends and friends of friends and of perfect strangers who have volunteered to share their own tales of caregiving.

The goal of the book is, first, to validate caregivers' actions, however insufficient and inadequate they might appear to be, to the caregiver reading the book and, then, to enliven what are often, if not always, sad, sorrowful and miserable situations by relating stories about the caregiving "crazies," which is our term for the countless unpredictable situations that are mindboggling at the time but hilarious in retrospect. Appropriate references to sources available for caregivers' needs are integrated into the narrative and supplemented in the Appendix, but this is a book to be read like a letter or conversation with friends who share your concerns and who can closely relate to your experiences. In other words, this is not a "self-help" book. It is intended to be a book of "self-soothing" that is both informative and entertaining.

AN INTRODUCTORY NOTE FROM ILENE

The experience of caring for an aging spouse or parent can best be described as bittersweet, reflecting a range of often conflicting experiences—sometimes deeply rewarding, other times deeply disturbing. Many of the more disturbing issues that I have encountered could have been mitigated by more careful planning; however, continuity of care planning has never achieved the same centrality as financial or estate planning in our culture. Why is that? I have asked myself that question so many times.

In my efforts to stimulate interest in the study of aging among my reluctant graduate students, I would advise them to imagine the older person they would wish to become and to work backward. In that way, I tried to make the aging experience more relevant to the here—and—now of even the very young. Most of these efforts "crash landed" or were met with deafening silence, but some of my students acknowledged that I might just be a "wise fool," and they were able to incorporate old age into a life span perspective, instead of writing off the years beyond age fifty-five as having no practical importance to them. Admittedly, in my youth, thirty was the age of obsolescence, so maybe there has been some progress.

What has been particularly more distressing to me, however, is the general resistance I have encountered to planning for retirement and beyond, not only among members of my parents' generation but also among members of my own age group. Considering the findings of a 2019 study undertaken for the federal Department of Health and Human Services, this trend becomes even more troubling. These data suggest that about 70 percent of older adults will need help from family caregivers or paid aides or some combination of both. So what's the reluctance?

Some of it has to do with human nature. Who wants to think about being old and frail when you are young or youngish and strong? Much of the resistance has to do with societal denial of the issues associated with an aging population with inevitable and widespread custodial needs. We are not much into social planning in this country until the problem becomes so grave that avoidance is no longer an option. We are the land of rugged individualism, and we live by the increasingly popular mantra "It's my personal choice" or, in Victorian terms, "The Englishman's right to be dirty."

So that brings us to this book. Maybe you feel you should have done a better job of preparing for the demands, including expense, of caregiving. I say join the crowd! This book is designed to grab your interest with firsthand accounts of caregivers and some honest facts about aging and caregiving. I am limiting the focus to caring for the aged, and the chapters that follow are constructed to provide support and safeguards to counteract the effects of anticipated failures. I consider some common issues that cause fireworks to go off when dealing with aging parents and spouses: "Broaching the Idea of Taking Away the Car Keys," "Broaching the Idea of Clearing out the

House," "Broaching the Idea of Selling the House," "Caregiving up Close, Caregiving at a Distance," "Challenges of Navigating Medical Care," "Broaching the Idea of Moving to Assisted Living," "The Challenges of Nursing Home Care," "The Challenges of Finding Paid Caregivers," "Show Me the Money: Paying for It," "What Happens to Caregivers When the Elder Goes off the Rails?" "Who Is Going to Take Care of Me?"

I have already been introduced as the gerontologist/daughter, and I would only add that among all the people who have refused to listen to me, my parents get the prize for being least attentive to any unsolicited advice from their daughter, "the professor." I have been through many caregiving experiences in my various roles, e.g., health proxy with parents and other older adult dependents, caring professional helping my clients and patients manage personal challenges and friend and confidante to many others who have experienced the stresses of managing the needs of older adults.

As already mentioned, this book is not so much about self-help as it is about self-soothing. The first goal is to offer validation of the emotional complexities associated with caregiving and some insight into how some people have resolved particular issues, especially those that no amount of planning could have prevented from arising. I hope this book offers to some readers a greater capacity for risk reduction not only in their current situation but also in their own aging experience.

CHAPTER 1

First Signs

Anyone who has had primary responsibility for caring for a dependent parent or spouse can vividly recall the first signs of impending distress. The red flags seem to come out of nowhere although you have had this feeling that something was going to happen and probably preferred to push any warning signs to the back recesses of your already overworked mind.

Caregiving creeps up on you. It often starts at the point that you need to broach the subject of "taking away the car keys" after the latest fender bender or parking scrape. Regarding the latter, you find a note from the irate owner of the car in front of your mother's vehicle telling you that someone witnessed the incident and shame on your mother for not reporting it. You call the number on the note and apologize and say that your mother wouldn't have ignored her responsibility but was probably unaware. Then you realize to your chagrin that unconsciousness is even worse than unaccountability.

In case you missed it, the car owner tells you, "Even more reason to take away the keys."

Easier said than done! Let's look at the situation of Mildred. Mildred suffered from a degenerative eye disease. She kept driving. When challenged, she said, "I know the roads," as if she could feel her way to her destination. After her daughter recovered from the shock of this ridiculous statement, she fumbled for a response. Ever try reasoning with a recalcitrant older person facing increasing functional limitations? Does this sound familiar? I won't give away quite yet how this was ultimately resolved lest you think reason immediately prevailed.

Also, lest you think the above is a one-shot deviation from the norm, almost the exact words were expressed by Charles, who, suffering from failing eyesight associated with advanced diabetes, insisted that he could drive to the local market to pick up his favorite carry-out because he "knew where it was!" Woe to anyone who challenged that particular leap from reality. In addition, Charles was driving without a license, knowing that if he went to get it renewed, he would fail the eye test.

Then there is the example of William, who decided he needed a new car after acknowledging the cosmetic challenges of his multi-bashed set of wheels. This he could acknowledge, but certainly not his own increasingly restrictive mobility resulting from an advanced arthritic condition. William was famous for saying, "The only time that I feel normal is when I am driving." Bad enough that his own judgment was clouded, he sneaked off to a local car dealership, hobbled out of his car and purchased a new car without anyone questioning his capacity to drive. Understood—disability is not cause for depriving anyone of the right to drive; however, when the person is of extreme advanced age and almost plowed into another car at the dealership while pulling into the parking lot and then needed assistance walking into the showroom, one has to wonder about the reasonableness of the ensuing sale. The lesson here is that, in a free society, you, the caregiver, are likely to get little or no help from anyone else in constraining your resistant relative.

I say relative because the likelihood is that you are either William's spouse or child, most likely the daughter. When you start out on this journey, you probably will be going it on your own. William didn't give up his driving until he couldn't get into the car without assistance, which was not, as you can expect, readily forthcoming. Somehow, there were no dire consequences in this instance, unless you consider the fact that his wife's blood pressure shot through the roof and his daughter developed ulcers.

It is important to note that members of "The Greatest Generation" are living well into their nineties, even hundreds. Their own parents very often lived fairly independently until their deaths. The prospect of losing independence for any substantial length of time was limited. But hey, good, strong constitutions and modern medicine have resulted in caregiving crises never before experienced. The combination of increased longevity and failure to plan is quite the formula for increasing the odds of confronting caregiving consternation. Why would you plan when there was no precedent for it other than to depend on informal (family) support throughout your life?

Taking the example of William one step further, his children made efforts to have him and Bernice, his wife, move to assisted living years before the car became the lightning rod for unwanted intervention. The family was fortunate to have more than adequate resources to afford assisted living, which, we realize, is not an option for many families. In addition, such a move would at least have avoided any doubts about continuum of care and provided some peace of mind for the future, since the assisted living would have been part of a continuing life care community. William and Bernice would have no part of that. William told Bernice, after an incident in which she had broken his fall with her own body and in the process fractured her pelvis, "We do not have to listen to our children." Of course not! You only have to go to them when the situation devolves to the point that all hope for maintaining independence is gone. Even then you don't have to necessarily appreciate any efforts, because your children are only fulfilling their filial responsibility.

Getting back to Mildred, to her credit, she chose to go to an assisted living facility and stopped driving when sympathetically asked, "How would you feel if you hurt someone in an accident?" Assisted living is not a complete answer to caregiving concerns but, in many cases, offers some degree of certainty and reassurance to families who can afford the expense. Another big IF!

I will get to the various options for caregiving later. For now, suffice it to say we suffer from too little continuity of care planning, not to mention too few resources and too much burden on family members, particularly, spouses and daughters, to carry the load, no matter how lovingly and graciously.

Charles' denial of reality did not end favorably. While the aforementioned "Mother," who was caught in the act of "brushing" the car in front of her, and Mildred both reluctantly turned over the keys, Charles refused to do so. Just as William would have steadfastly refused to do if not hog-tied by his disabilities. Is this greater need to maintain independence a man thing or at least a generational pitfall of masculine socialization? Charles predeceased his stubborn refusal to "see" the error of his ways, narrowly escaping an arguably worse fate of taking along with him some innocent victim, unless you consider the loss of sleep and constant angst of his sister and close friends, who felt powerless to intervene despite the blazing hazard signs. The last resort for his sister would have been to notify the police or Adult Protective Services. It doesn't take much imagination to grasp the anguish associated with that prospect. Sometimes it takes tough love. She was on the verge of making that call.

To be fair, some people facing increasing frailty do make the call to "give up the keys," but I wouldn't bet on it, and it's usually not automatic. Leon, who was notorious for *asking* for back seat driving assistance, such as "Is it okay for me to pull out?" ultimately decided on his own to curtail his automotive adventures, but it still had to be on his terms!

Sometimes you can "depend on the kindness of strangers" in reining in your loved one in volatile situations. Case in point—John, who had early-stage Alzheimer's, got hold of the keys to the car and went AWOL. When John stopped for gas approximately four hours and one state later, an observant filling station attendant picked up on John's disorientation and nipped John's road trip in the bud, much to his chagrin. John, unsurprisingly, was in denial about his condition while his wife Maria had been coping with his advancing dementia to the best of her ability.

Do not mistake this commentary as an admonition against keeping older drivers on the road. In a recent article in the *New York Times* (October 19, 2021), Jane Brody provides evidence that drivers over age seventy and older are less likely to be involved in a fatal car accident than younger drivers. Other data reveal that drivers aged seventy and over have fewer crashes reported to the police than middle age drivers. In her piece, however, Brody quotes Dr. Louise Aronson, a geriatrician at the University of California, San Francisco, who states that, in order to justify continuing to drive, "older people may tell others they don't go farther than the grocery store, they stay off the highway or they don't drive at night," and that "such comments can be a red flag that it is time to stop driving altogether." Driving is important to older people, and being older is associated with better safety records, but, if and when the need arises to take away the keys, we need to keep our loved ones protected on the road.

There will be a first sign of progressing need, although gratefully not always related to diminishing mental capacity. It may take the form of the need to broach the subject of taking away the keys or accompanying the spouse or parent on doctors' visits. It may take the form of increased need for assistance with activities of daily living, beginning with shopping and cleaning. There may be multiple first signs that ultimately lead to increased burden and stress on the caregiver. How many daughters have given up their independence to take care of their parents? There are endless examples of women who have had to give up their jobs in order to be available to meet parental or spousal needs. Women with their own families often find themselves juggling the demands of a job and two households. They truly are sandwiched between child care and parental needs and requirements.

The idea is to not wait for the first signs of abundant need but to make some prearrangements. Even so as I develop the different themes in this book, you will discover that the options are limited and there is really no perfect scenario; well, forget perfect, there is no ideal solution. There are courageous and creative compromises, as I will demonstrate, even for William, Bernice and their disregarded daughter Ginny.

Caregiving for most is an adventure into the unknown reaches of relationship and practical survival. Those who come out of this experience best are able to see the signs and then take the steps necessary to resolve the challenges as they emerge. It's a process.

Advice to those who are seeing the first signs follows:

Do not panic.

1. Reach out for any support and validation from trusted friends and gerontological and legal professionals. Read some of the books and articles listed in the Appendix, which will guide you to some resources provided by agencies or the government and which also provide insight on how certain recurring issues might be handled by caregivers.

2. Try, of course, to communicate your concerns with your dependent spouse or parent or siblings, but just don't be surprised when you don't get any cooperation.

In the next chapter, I delve into the issue of "the house," a powerful symbol of the inner psychic state and practical nightmare.

CHAPTER 2

The House, the Home

Psychologists have long had a field day with the house as a metaphor for the mind: a neatly organized house is representative of a neatly functioning psyche. Well, actually who would argue with the practicality and the aesthetic pleasure of living in a well-ordered home or its symbolic comparison to a well-ordered mind?

Brian Collinson (Vibrant Jung Thing Blog, 2017), a psychotherapist and Jungian analyst, explores the symbolism of home in its many aspects, including associations with a sense of belonging, safety and contentment, and he identifies the connection between finding oneself and finding a home, among other themes.

If the car is a symbol of independence, and taking away the keys deprives an aging adult of his or her freedom, removing that adult from his or her home is like stripping away security, not just shelter, but discarding memories related to the home and its contents.

I don't wish to belabor this because I think the point is clear; however, the house is more than a dwelling place. You only begin to see clearly the deep-seated implications of that statement when you threaten a dependent person with removal from a cherished habitat.

Let us begin with the aforementioned example of William and Bernice. They weren't budging from their rental apartment and refused to consider any options until and unless forced by circumstance. The rental aspect is significant in demonstrating that home proprietorship has nothing to do with home connectedness. In my experience, as dependency grows, so grows the need to stay rooted wherever it is you hang your hat. In the case of William and Bernice, they made no attempt to accommodate the apartment to meet the requirements for managing William's advancing arthritic condition. Despite efforts by Ginny and her brother to motivate the couple to take some steps toward assisted living in a life care community, the couple remained rooted to the spot, both psychologically and physically. Ironically, because of failure to move, William and Bernice were faced with the only option of nursing home placement for William. The apartment could not be modified to meet his extreme needs for care, and although Bernice resisted the choice for residential care for her husband, having promised him that she would never "put him in a nursing home," the decision was eventually taken out of their hands.

Perhaps William and Bernice represent an extreme example of failure to move, because they stayed in the rental for over sixty years while others in their social network made the move to Florida upon retirement, a popular option at the time. Some became snowbirds and went back and forth, and others chose to stay in Florida. Still others eventually moved back "home" to be nearer to their families. The old adage about children coming home when they need you applies to aging parents coming home to their families, as life expectancy continues to increase. Home, after all, is "where the heart is."

When those who depend upon our care remain in their own home, there are all kinds of practical issues that need to be addressed. Take the example of Charlotte and Tom, for whom their marriage represented a second commitment. They married later in life after both had served as principal caregiver for their predeceased spouses. When, in their late seventies, they tied the knot, they decided to reside in Charlotte's house. They added a room so that Tom could have his private space. Things went well for a number of years. Charlotte's daughter, Janet, a practicing physician, would visit them regularly in Florida. She started getting palpitations as the years went by, and the rate of accumulation of "purchases" hit skyrocketing proportions. She was known to say, "How am I ever going to be able to clean out that house if they move . . . or, to put it delicately, move on?"

The time came when, in this case, the couple decided that they needed to move to assisted living. They reached that decision when it became obvious that they could not manage on their own at home. That point had been made abundantly clear to Janet on one of her visits when she discovered cans and jars of food piled high in the master bedroom closet. This storage nightmare was only brought to her attention by her sheepish mother and Tom, because Charlotte and Tom did not know what to do about the mess from the open bottle of soy sauce that had spilled all over everything in the closet. Just imagine what it was like to clean up sticky soy sauce from a carpet as well as the clothing in that closet. Some of those cans had expiration dates from five years back. That incident wasn't the immediate catalyst for the decision to go to assisted living, but for a short period of time, Charlotte and Tom did agree to have someone help with the shopping and cleaning. That's another thing: home proprietorship for many means, "Don't touch my stuff."

They would not let the aide clean their personal space or assist with any personal care or meals, but they complained that "she doesn't do anything." They complained about the cost, even though the aide came only for three hours a couple of times a week. Charlotte's functional limitations exceeded those of Tom, which ultimately resulted in his awakening to the need for assisted living, with full support and encouragement of his sons. Charlotte was less disposed toward the move, but she recognized the toll that independent living was taking on her husband. Reconciliation did not occur without objection from the different "camps." Janet, the most engaged of all the couple's children, managed to maintain equanimity in the face of controversy. Janet left it up to her mother and Tom to make their own decision but explored various options. She found what seemed like a very good assisted living facility in the vicinity of their home and took them to visit. They approved of it, and Janet came up with a plan first to sell her mother's house and then make arrangements for the move.

Such planning was not in their repertoire. One day they decided to pay a visit to the facility and, in the process, signed a contract to move at the beginning of the next month. Janet was astonished by their action, and she couldn't believe that they were planning on vacating the house before it was sold, leaving her with the enormous task of simultaneously arranging their move, clearing out the house and selling the house. The other adult children, all male, left primary responsibility to her. We will get to issues associated with the particular burden on women in a later chapter.

The only point to be made here is that, although Janet was "surprised" by the impulsiveness of this act, this display of "independence" is hardly unique among older people with growing dependency.

Examples of this behavior abound. Clara lived in the same house all her married life. Her husband predeceased her, and she was bound and determined to "stay put." One day, in what also is not an atypical situation, she accidentally turned on the oven when she had intended to light one of the burners to boil some water. Well, actually she did both. But she didn't notice the oven was on until the Tupperware in the oven caught fire and the blaze took hold throughout the kitchen. Fortunately, Clara's daughter was in the house at the time and the fire department arrived in time to salvage the house, but the process of putting out the fire created tremendous water damage. Nobody was hurt. Clara's house was deemed uninhabitable, and she moved "temporarily" to a small apartment. She initially planned on going back to the house, but after the renovation, she didn't recognize it and was more amenable to a permanent move. But all of this "reasonable" behavior did not occur spontaneously. First, upon seeing that her daughters had packed up a lot of her belongings to make room for the renovation, she insisted that they put everything back where she left it. Being dutiful daughters, they complied! Later, Clara decided she did not need so much room any longer and decided to move into a facility that offered different levels of care instead of remaining independently in a smaller space. Clara adjusted and progressed through the different levels of care until her passing at the age of 100—a success story, yes, but nonetheless fraught with some nail-biting tension.

Not every older person is reluctant to make a change. Although for most change is difficult, some people embrace change. One such example stands out. Richard and Carol picked up and moved to a supervised independent living community when Carol determined "it was time." They would be proactive and not wait until a crisis. They made the move during the Covid pandemic to a luxury residence and then, not being able to tolerate all the restrictions, moved to another residence with more liberal policies regarding residents' behavior, such as those related to their comings and goings. That second move met the couple's capacity for tolerance for another couple of months. Carol and Richard are now safely and happily ensconced in their own apartment once again.

Some people make the move voluntarily, usually when faced with some functional limitations or to avoid becoming a burden to their children. Mildred sold her home after the death of her husband whom she had taken care of for years. She didn't need the space anymore, and she suffered from failing eyesight. Ben, who also had lost his beloved spouse and suffered mild infirmity associated with a chronic heart condition, decided to move to assisted living in his adopted state of Florida. Both of these individuals wanted to remain as independent as possible. As good fortune would have it, Ben met a woman with whom he formed a close friendship. When her children encouraged her to move to an assisted living community near where they lived, both she and Ben made the move together. Ben enjoyed his remaining years in close companionship with a lovely woman and her family. Ben had the attitude that assisted living afforded him the opportunity to retain control over his life. He did not see it as a restriction on his autonomy.

Most people probably back into making some move from their own home. Perhaps that's best; it cuts down on the ambivalence, although it may place a strain on children who have to yield to the uncertainty of allowing the process to play itself out. Therein lies the rub! In addition, there is always the risk that increasing frailty will reduce the availability of options. Some supportive residential communities require the applicant to be able to walk or at least use a walker or wheelchair independently or, otherwise, be deemed ineligible for the level of care provided.

Some people can't afford the option of independent or assisted living. It's generally expensive. So many of our choices are tied in with socioeconomic factors, including cultural priorities. These themes will be elaborated in a later chapter.

The need for caregiving support is ubiquitous, and eventually almost every family faces the question of how best to provide care for Mom and Dad. Many families take a parent into their home or build an addition for Mom or Dad before any real issues emerge. Sometimes, the parent decides to return to their original community, finding the change in locale unacceptable. Sometimes a child may move in with a parent, and if the child is dependent on the parent, complications are almost certain to arise from this mutual dependency. In cases of financial dependency, there is always the risk of financial malfeasance. There is no blueprint or "one size fits all." It is often beneficial to remain flexible and open to adjustments.

Not everybody faces "the move." It is important to note that older people predominantly remain in the community, in their original home or in a home they downsized to in mid-life. They age in place, but when there is a move, there will be hurdles for caregivers to overcome.

THE PHYSICAL MOVE

We turn our attention to some experiences with downsizing and clearing out the house physically. Yes, moving not only has its psychological aspects, but it is replete with practical considerations and challenges that rock the very foundation of any caregiver's constitution.

We return to Janet, who had been left with the sole responsibility for arranging her parents' move, cleaning and selling the house. After adjusting to the initial shock, Janet, with her mother's and stepfather's reluctant approval, arranged for a moving service that specialized in downsizing. In several meetings with the lovely and very patient owner of the company, Charlotte and Tom reluctantly went through clothes and other possessions to make decisions about what they wanted to take with them to assisted living. A move date was arranged with the assisted living facility, and on that date, Charlotte and Tom vacated the house with select furniture and personal possessions. Deciding what to leave behind turned into a heated dispute, but better judgment ultimately prevailed. The couple left for their new home on the day of departure, merrily waving Janet off. In coming days, they would make continuous requests for "more of their stuff" including a stepping machine, which would have been the undoing of both of them if they had actually attempted to use it.

Janet put the house up for sale, but that would take time. She finally got Charlotte and Tom to agree to a garage sale to help clear out the excessive number of remaining items that were of no particular interest to anyone. Charlotte and Tom had multiple sets of kitchen appliances, utensils, equipment, dishes as well as closets filled to the max with underutilized clothing and shoes. The final blow to Janet's generally high level of composure was the garage, or rather what she discovered there. Cartons of decorations for every holiday, even some holidays she had trouble identifying, lined the walls, leaving very little room to spare. Except for the overflow of household, garden and automotive tools, which were hanging from every conceivable opening in the walls up to the rafters, the only thing not there was a car. What to do?

Janet told Charlotte that she was having a garage sale once she got a handle on all of the stuff. The demands for more personal items increased. Most of the stuff was Charlotte's, and she finally agreed to the sale. Sale day finally arrived, and the couple insisted upon being on site, which would have been risky considering the challenges of wading through the rummage. Also to be considered was the emotional plight sure to be associated with the loss of personal things. Janet put her foot down and told the couple not to attempt to come. They had left the matter in her hands and she did not think it wise for them to be there. That created a temporary breach in a loving mother-daughter relationship, but it clearly illustrates that, at some point, the caregiver needs either to take charge or be pushed off an emotional cliff.

The drama did not stop there. After the garage sale, the couple insisted that the remaining items be put in storage for their reappraisal. Their wishes were respectfully granted. Janet survived the challenges but at a cost to her equanimity and also to her medical practice, which needed to be accommodated as well. Janet did have help from some friends, especially one local resident who kept her eye on things when Janet returned home.

The sale of the house took longer than expected but eventually took place. You might say "case closed" but for one loose end. Janet faced almost the same exact predicament a couple of years later with her brother, another family pack rat who needed her to clean up after him. Is it any wonder that Janet is a very organized individual? An unsung heroine!

As stated, moving does not always mean moving into a supervised setting. In Bernice's case, after the passing of her husband William, her children were surprised at her willingness to purchase a co-op in a "better" neighborhood. Their surprise was predicated upon the realization that a long-held belief in Bernice's hesitancy to budge was in fact a family myth. Bernice had deferred to her husband all of their married life and was eager to have for the first time in her life, at the age of eighty-eight, a home of her own. The move was orchestrated by Ginny and a close friend with skill in home design. A proper first "reveal" was planned, and Bernice, in absolute amazement, walked in on a completed project: her first private residence, replete with all of her original furniture and accoutrements! She was awestruck and couldn't believe that what she was seeing was all of her original items rearranged to fit the dimensions of this new space, which was to become her "forever" home. As her needs for caregiving grew, they were incrementally accommodated through home care, a different option for resolution of caregiving concerns. Had William been more amenable to moving and modifying his home to meet his growing needs, he may never have needed to go to the nursing home where he spent his final days.

But that takes planning! Obviously, private arrangements come with different, generally greater, demands on informal caregivers, which will be elaborated in Chapter 3. It's the planning, or shall we say non-planning, piece of this story that is addressed next.

OTHER PRACTICAL CONSIDERATIONS THAT NOBODY WANTS TO KNOW ABOUT

I like to refer to the following as the "Twelve Facts to Face in Curing Caregiving Incognizance" or, in other words, what you need to know at least to wake up to the realities of aging in America.

1. We have no universal long-term care policy in this country.

2. Only 2 percent of older people are in assisted living facilities and 4.5 percent are in nursing homes.

3. A great majority of older adults over the age of sixty-five reside in the community.

4. Only 7 percent of adults over fifty in this country have long-term care insurance.

5. Lack of long-term care coverage can devastate one's financial plan.

6. Medicaid eligibility for either home care or residential care is income and asset based.

7. In order to qualify for Medicaid eligibility for nursing home care or home health care, you are forced to pay penalties on excess income or assets. Medicaid does NOT cover assisted living.

8. There are certain protections for assets, but rules are becoming more stringent with regard to transfers in relation to Medicaid home care eligibility in even the more liberal state of New York, where the look-back period on transfers changed from no look-back to thirty months, as compared to five years in most states.

9. The home generally is an exempt asset in eligibility for Medicaid coverage for community health care, but typically for the life of the Medicaid recipient, the spouse or, in some cases, a child who resides in the home and provides care.

10. The need to plan with an elder attorney is paramount in avoiding impoverishing either a spouse or a dependent child in securing any government support.

11. The need to plan with an elder attorney is paramount—period.

12. The designated informal caregiver is the linchpin in managing caregiving needs given the fragmentation in the long-term care system.

I stated earlier that it is important not to panic, unless of course you are the designated informal caregiver on whose back the burden of responsibility falls. Then you can panic, but "get over it!" It helps to know you are in good company with approximately 80 percent of the over-sixty-five population and approximately 70 percent of the over-eighty population remaining in place in the community. We Americans are a resourceful people. We just need to adjust to new demands.

The ensuing chapters demonstrate how creatively people have been managing despite all of the challenges. The only suggestion I make is that, if you are ahead of the curve, talk with an elder attorney! Talk with an elder attorney especially if you feel you are behind the eight-ball! TALK WITH AN ELDER ATTORNEY! We will return to the subject of "Paying for Care" in a later chapter and how some of our contributors have survived that difficult task. Money issues are certainly among the most significant, but they are only a part of the caregiving conundrum.

Chapter 3, "Staying at Home: Caregiving Up Close, Caregiving from a Distance," follows next; makes sense since home is where most of us choose to remain. Generally, these situations involve creative juggling of responsibilities among professionals and informal caregivers alike. The maxim "it takes a village" most certainly applies.

CHAPTER 3

Staying at Home: Caregiving Up Close, Caregiving from a Distance

By now it should be pretty clear that inertia is the rule of thumb when it comes to caregiving. The dilemma facing most people is how to maintain the status quo and manage any limitations that accompany old age without having to make any major changes. In other words, "I don't want to think about it if I don't have to," even though the inevitable may lurk somewhere in the distant recesses of the unconscious. This is not to say that people don't think that they are planning, at least financially, for any increasing demands that are likely to accompany the passing of years. It's just that, in my experience, it is the rare attorney, financial adviser or accountant that actually considers the cost implications of continuity of care as a major life altering experience. Therefore, the dual influences of avoidance and ignorance generally result in the popular reactive approach to continuity of care planning. Care planning done right is more than just planning financially, and all the money in the world will not protect the designated informal caregiver from the customary challenges of managing the needs of one's dependent spouse or parent in the home.

PREDICTABLE CHALLENGES

When we last left off with Bernice, she had moved into her "forever home" after the loss of her husband for whom she was the principal caregiver for many years. Ginny and her brother Scott had done their homework and, after meeting with an elder law attorney, determined that Bernice should purchase a home for multiple reasons, including the fact that a home is an exempt asset in determining eligibility for community home care under the Medicaid regulations in their home state. The family learned quite a bit about the need to think ahead from the experience of nursing home placement for William, husband and father. Determined not to make the same mistakes again, some forethought was also given to the inevitability of Bernice's growing need for assistance with basic activities of daily living such as feeding, bathing, dressing and walking and instrumental activities of daily living such as cooking, cleaning, transportation and managing finances. Bernice was still very independent, and it was easy to gloss over potential challenges with a general assurance that services could be incorporated on an as-needed basis. At the time there was no look-back associated with transferring assets in determining eligibility for community Medicaid for home care so the coast was clear should the need for home care arise. Both Ginny and Scott, convinced that nursing home placement would never be an option for their mother, left the remaining assets in their mother's name. Nobody really knows what is going to happen, but in this case, the family did consider the alternatives and attempt to make reasonable choices.

And so, true to Robert Burns, "The best-laid plans of mice and men often go awry," circumstances did not exactly work out as smoothly as would have been desired.

They forgot about factoring Bernice into the equation. They didn't exactly forget. They fell into a state of blissful denial. Bernice woke them up to the reality of her intransigence at every turn. Recall the incident with the car from Chapter 1. Bernice only gave up the keys after her minor fender benders made her a pariah on her own turf. Bernice would only allow one person, her husband's male caregiver, to provide any assistance with shopping or cleaning or anything not personal. That worked for quite a few years until the need for assistance with personal care arose. Every shift in her requirements and associated recommendation for remediation resulted in renewed rebelliousness.

Bernice's response was not unique. Clara managed to conceal from her daughter the fact that she was having trouble walking, for a long time. She struggled to go food shopping using a walker for some support. Her daughter discovered the walker by accident and, upon further inquiry, learned the extent of the immobility issue. Clara, as it turned out, needed hip surgery but, because of her dogged determination to go it alone, chose to suffer rather than subject herself to her daughter's direction.

Often it is the spouse providing the care for a husband or wife. Somehow expectations made of spouses may fit more into the generally accepted norm, and so many a beleaguered, albeit loving spouse, has the privilege of being nurse, companion and devoted servant to an appreciative, but still, demanding partner. I didn't say it, but most often it being the woman providing the personal care, it is not hard to understand the stereotypical root of a husband's expectations. I know "the times they are a changing," but not quite yet! Louise is an example of a loving wife who has tirelessly been caring for her husband, who suffers from a degenerative neurological disease. She doesn't complain, but she is tired. She and her husband, Dan, decided to compound their difficulties by adopting a second dog, because clearly one wasn't enough. They had to go out and buy a new recliner because the new, rather large, puppy took over Dan's favorite chair. Dan wanted the dog and Louise complied because she loves her husband; and, besides, what's one more joyful addition to a perfectly disordered existence? The couple is making the best of their situation. Yet, this example raises the question: what is the cost to the one providing the care?

There is a difference between overseeing care and directly providing care.

DIFFERENT STROKES FOR DIFFERENT FOLKS

Not every caregiver is the same. However, most are women and most are either spouses or daughters. Most caregiving in this country is provided by informal caregivers. Some are paid under long-term care insurance plans or government programs. Under relatively new eligibility requirements, family members of Medicaid recipients can be reimbursed, but rules differ from state to state, and the spouse is generally exempt from participation. Nevertheless, programs such as CDPAP NY (Consumer Directed Personal Assistance Program) has allowed people to hire and manage their own caregivers. It's not much of a stretch to understand that this is a less costly option for the state and also does not afford the same professional oversight and backup coverage as available through a home health care provider, but for many families, it is a practical solution to caregiving challenges: at once giving informal caregivers remuneration for their work and care recipients the freedom to choose aides.

Perhaps not unexpectedly, I have had more than one *formal* caregiver tell me that she would prefer to work for someone other than her own mother. One told me she had much more patience for managing a non-family member's "crazies" than those of her own mother. I must admit this came as a source of great reassurance to me in my "oversight" role as the designated informal caregiver for my mother and her brother, as well as my father before them. I have always wondered about my limitations as a daughter and niece when thrown into a tailspin over some personal care responsibility or predictable demonstration of resistance from the relative under care. I have developed a tremendous respect for the paid caregivers who have the lion's share of direct care responsibility for my charges. Many of the women filling the role of home health aide are from other cultures, primarily Caribbean, South Asian and African, in my experience. I have wondered what makes them give so generously of themselves to strangers in a strange land, and without overstating the point, I have come to believe that they have a deep sense of high regard for their work, which is more than work to them. My uncle can be difficult, and yet two Jamaican women have provided direct care for him for over three years, and one told me that she feels that God sent this man to her to care for and that she believes that this was a trust that she would fulfill. After, I stopped crying from relief, mostly for myself, because I couldn't believe that I was so fortunate to have this support and might get some freedom from the constant demands. I should add that, when one of these dedicated aides takes a vacation, the other fills in, strictly voluntarily. I had to acknowledge that these women were better than I am.

I have heard it all. They have their job. I have mine. Only theirs is more important. I have oversight and I am tired, but they find dignity in providing care to people, and that is nothing short of heroic. They are women. They will admit that, in their countries, their work is considered women's work. If you need help in the Dominican Republic, according to one of my sources, another friend or family member will step in to assist for a little while, even though, just as in this country, the primary responsibility generally falls to a wife or daughter. Men help in other ways, not unlike here. But these women don't seem to resent or regret their role, and I wonder what we are losing in this country as kinship networks dissolve and financial imperatives preoccupy our every thought and action. Here women try hard not to let the burden of the responsibility diminish their satisfaction in their caregiving role, but the burden can become too much for many, resulting in feelings of inadequacy.

So what is funny about this, or at least mildly amusing? Well, the funny thing to me is, the more things change, the more they stay the same! Men take care of a lot, but it's not the same.

Bill regularly visits his mother and makes home repairs. Rob takes care of financial management for his mother. John did his mother's food shopping and took her to doctors' appointments. Steve lived with his ninety-three-year-old mother after his divorce, and although she had some formal home care, he sometimes wound up giving his mother a bath, in addition to regularly making her meals, doing the cleaning and shopping. Of course, note, Steve was living with his mother, and therefore this situation was a bit of an anomaly. But this just proves that roles are not set in stone. Only, they are still pretty much set. Wouldn't it be glorious if the reward and responsibilities of caregiving were truly shared between the sexes and family and formal caregivers more highly valued? This is difficult to achieve in a society bound by the ideal of "rugged individualism" or a belief in independence from state or government assistance. Gender based biases that devalue the work of caregiving also serve as constraints against progress. Although beyond the scope of this writing, our sociopolitical structure directly impacts the American aging experience and our respective caregiving contributions.

For now, men give in different ways, and husbands fill gaps in direct service for dependent wives. But we still breathe a sigh of relief when we know there is a daughter hanging from the family tree, waiting to be called to duty to assist her aging dad with caring for her aging mom.

CAREGIVING TIMELINE

Caregiving tends to follow a pattern. I previously stated that it creeps up on you slowly, and that generally is the case in situations involving aging parents or spouses.

It usually starts with the necessity to assist the increasingly dependent individual with small tasks such as shopping, cleaning or accompanying to doctors' visits. Not much of a hurdle for most newly anointed caregivers. Often there is a division of labor, with men assisting a parent with home repairs, for example, and women assisting with household responsibilities. There is no fixed timeframe for this phase; however, once your loved one is no longer capable of self-transport, you can expect the needs to increase. Also, chronic health issues are likely to compound with time, leading to increased demand for assistance with daily activities.

Many people are able to keep up a high level of independence as they age as long as they maintain executive function or the ability to select and monitor behaviors that facilitate the achievement of

their goals. Some people are hampered by traditional gender socialization that emphasized different skill development for girls and
boys. The over-ninety-year-old man who can sew is still a novelty,
unless the gentleman in question is a tailor or a surgeon perhaps?
Hand coordination is likely to be the root of any technical difficulties for older men as well as women in areas requiring precise man-
ual dexterity. Many men are very skilled in the kitchen just as many
older women can write a check, but I have known women who had
to learn to write a check when faced with the loss of their husbands.
Many sons (and daughters) of older women take on the responsibility of managing their finances, because it's easier than teaching an
"old woman new tricks." Some men as well as women gladly turn
over their financial management to a trusted child or close relative,
if not a professional. At ninety, or even earlier, they may not want to
be bothered. I think most people reaching old age (sixty-five-plus)
today in this country have mastered basic living skills or know where
to turn to get a rip in the seat of their pants repaired or their budget
balanced. Therefore, barring any significant cognitive dysfunction,
there is no reason for people not to remain in charge of their lives
throughout their lives, unless "they don't want to be bothered" or
they suffer from dementia or a related state of cognitive decline, a
sure-fire indicator of the progressing need for support, raising the
question—what now?

WHAT NOW?

The "what now" stage of caregiving generally is preceded by
either escalating physical disability or, as mentioned, escalating
mental disability or both. This stage is marked by increasing caregiving requirements in areas related to household management, personal care and coordination of services. Suddenly, the "designated

informal caregiver" finds herself swimming upstream against a torrent of micro and some macro demands for attention every day. Over the course of time, the need to help with the shopping becomes the need to do the shopping, as well as prepare the meals. The need to ensure car maintenance becomes the need to become the designated driver. The need to accompany your loved one to the doctor becomes the need to schedule the appointments, as well as implement any follow-up arrangements. Again, in situations in which physical challenges are the predominant obstacle to your loved one's independence, much of the planning and coordination of services can be managed by the aging individual. Having a mentally capable, although physically challenged, individual in your care is a boon to the caregiver, since, according to many informal caregivers, coordination of services can become almost as onerous a task as providing direct care.

Even in situations where there is no neurodegenerative disorder, such as Alzheimer's or Parkinson's, the advancing of years will bring about normative changes in cognitive activity and inhibitory control or, in other words, "frontal lobe" dysfunction. This is to be expected, and mother's increased lack of inhibition or dad's memory lapses will bring intrigue to the caregiving situation along with auditory, sensory and other age-related functional limitations.

Margaret was still living alone when her daughter Joan received a note from an irate neighbor complaining about a leak from the sink in Margaret's apartment that had resulted in damages. Fortunately, the problem could be traced to clogging in the drain that, thankfully, could be prevented with a mesh drain strainer. Margaret refused to acknowledge that she had dropped food down the drain, creating the clog, despite evidence to the contrary. On another occasion, fumes from her oven resulted in the activation of the smoke detector, which resulted in a visit from the local fire department. The "fuming," which could only be matched by Margaret's expression of outrage, was traced to the existence of food bits on the bottom of the stove. Little incidents like these resulted in Margaret being banned from the kitchen, at the age of ninety-eight. Of course, these things could happen to anyone, but people are known to have less patience with the very old and sometimes accuse them indiscriminately. In Margaret's case, she was exonerated from any responsibility for leakage from the radiator in her living room, for which she had also been blamed. Right is right, and fair is fair! Yes, Margaret's concentration may have lapsed, and it was perhaps best that she not be responsible for cleaning her non-self-clean oven or making sure her drains remain unclogged, and that is why, caregiving oversight took on greater necessity in her life. Pretty good to still have been living alone at ninety-eight, and even though Margaret had to observe some kitchen restrictions, Joan made every effort to support her independence. Ultimately, Margaret's needs surpassed Joan's ability to manage with just a few hours of paid home care, and gradually more home care was added, until eventually Margaret was receiving 24/7 paid home care.

Joan's roles as "supervisor," "daughter," "majordomo" are still intact. Joan now has professional aides to assist with her mother's personal care but, otherwise, is responsible for running her mother's household (with Margaret's approval), as well as her own.

Joan's experience is paralleled by many designated informal caregivers who begin the caregiving route by providing limited services and then gradually find themselves having to introduce paid home care to supplement their activities, if they can afford it! Very often the one receiving care does not take to these additions with gratitude or grace. The added support is often viewed as an encumbrance and strongly and loudly resisted. Exclamations of "You made me a prisoner in my own home" or "Get out; I don't need you!" are not uncommon. After the sixth home health aide has been sent packing because "she just sits and watches me," or in one case the care recipient kept resorting to calling the police to remove the home health aide, it can be expected that the designated caregiver will reach the limit of tolerance and endurance. Designated informal caregivers become familiar with unsolicited advice regarding how to try to soothe the concerns of the one under their care. I have found that approach to be largely futile. Others report similar results.

Naturally, people want to be reassured that they are not losing control over their lives, but it is hard, if not impossible, to encourage acts of independence in individuals whose needs are outpacing their capacity for independent living. At some point, it may become vital to do some reality testing with your loved one and set some limits. I have sometimes been surprised at the response when options are clearly delineated and choices are placed in the care recipient's hands. In other words, "Do you want to remain at home?" Sometimes peace will prevail for short periods, but there will be peaks and valleys, and it is best to get used to the roller coaster ride.

CAREGIVING CONFLICTS

One can also anticipate internecine conflict. Sometimes there are disputes between different aides, such as in Lenore's situation in which her two paid aides quibbled over scheduling. Often the tension results from conflict over tasks. The DIC (designated informal caregiver) comes to depend on the existence of a routine that can be easily upset by the absence of a particular aide. In Lenore's case, the DIC was forced to intervene to resolve the scheduling conflict. Lenore tried to enforce order by registering her concern that she might not always be available to pick up the slack and that the aides needed to be able to work things out independently. Good luck with that! The DIC is in for the long haul, and the job draws some parallels to running a nursing home. Most would agree that conflicts are unavoidable. They can be reduced somewhat if the aides have clearly defined responsibilities and/or are associated with a home care agency that provides backup. But someone has to be available to assist the substitute, and sometimes the responsibility will fall to a surrogate, such as the DIC's brother or daughter, who, often having been recruited under duress, may not perform as well as one might hope.

Internecine conflicts are the rage among siblings or between spouse and children. The DIC may expect some extra direct support from a brother who "is handling the finances" and considers that to be the equivalent of "being on deck." Not so! One caregiving wife told her children that, if they didn't show up to help, she was leaving. Roles have to be worked out in these situations in order for tranquility to prevail, but easier said than done. Linda's mother Martha refused to move from her own home to live with her because she wanted to be near her son, who barely visited. Tamara, who lived in a different state than her parents, tried to get them to accept some home care, which they flatly refused. When she tried to get her brothers, who lived near her parents, to assist her in engaging some support for their parents, her brothers told Tamara to "mind your own business." Of course, Tamara understood that to mean that, at the first sign of difficulty, it would become her business. Speaking of business, when Theresa asked for some compensation for managing her parents' household and needs, her siblings told her "that can't be monetized."

Sometimes you can talk about these disputes and arrive at a sensible solution, but better to expect that the caregiving route will be fraught with difficulties and understand that one must carry on. If one plans effectively, one can reduce the disturbances but not eliminate them entirely.

In case you may be thinking that moving your loved one into your own home might represent a simpler solution, this arrangement typically requires a different set of adjustments. Some people modify their homes by adding an in-law apartment, sometimes referred to as a granny flat, to provide additional space for mom and/or dad. In an article from *Real Simple* (December 2021), entitled "Money Confidential: Tale of Two Aging Parents," Holly Robinson reflects the feelings of others who have chosen this route, in cautioning one to be prepared for an emotional adjustment, as well as changes in lifestyle requirements that may arise. For example, even though she and her husband made sure to create space for her mom, they hadn't been prepared for the wide disparity in their meal scheduling. When she and her husband sat down for a late breakfast after a Sunday morning run, her mother commented, "By the time I'm ready for lunch, the two of you will barely be done with breakfast." Mother liked to have an early breakfast, lunch and dinner, complicating joint meal preparation and delivery. Also, even though you love your parent, you may recognize that the new arrangement creates certain emotional boundary issues that you thought you resolved a long time ago. In Holly Robinson's case, she recognized that she and her mother did not see "eye to eye" on many topics, but the need for the move to her home resulted in large part from a shortage of affordable options as well as her deep regard for the woman who raised her, quelling some of her doubts about the arrangement. Variations in planning are often associated with finances, and more tasks will naturally accrue to informal caregivers when money is tight.

Just as some families grow geographically closer with increasing age-related dependency, others, for one reason or another, struggle with providing care from a distance.

CAREGIVING FROM A DISTANCE

Many things are debatable when it comes to caregiving. Is the burden of juggling work, personal responsibilities and caregiving more or less stressful than devoting yourself full time to the care of your dependent family member? I think it depends upon the caregiver's comfort level with the situation at hand. Financial imperatives often dictate choices in these situations. I have known women who left their jobs and moved in with an aging parent or had the parent move in with them. Some try to straddle the demands of two separate households and a job. Juggling is very stressful. Depending upon the relationship between the informal caregiver and the care recipient, the new-founded familiarity associated with caring for another person can be the source of tremendous stress. So, it depends. Everyone's tolerance level is different, and different stressors affect different people differently. Louise moved from New York City to the suburbs to live with her aging mother and told me that every day she would wake up homesick. She felt she had no other choice because of financial constraints. I will return to this issue of affordability in a later chapter, but that was Louise's perception and she made her choice, which also included early retirement. Self-sacrifice is a big part of caregiving, and although people don't want to admit it, because of their love and respect for the person or people under their care, many caregivers suffer from depression, in addition to fatigue or exhaustion. Caregivers are also aging as well as getting younger. Baby boomers caring for their very old parents also qualify as old themselves. Caregiving among millennial generation adults is on the rise because of the pandemic and generally higher risk factors for morbidity among people of color. There are no blueprints to guide performance of newly emerging social roles. Caregiving is very much a pioneering experience.

Caregiving from a distance has its own brand of baptism by fire. I can assure you that Sarah and Dominique never considered the future needs of their aging parents when each respectively got married and moved to the United States from Israel and France. No one would question their choice to relocate when they were in early adulthood. However, when you are the only daughter, you are likely to find yourself flying back and forth to manage parental needs and often unexpectedly. Dominique ultimately decided to leave her job to stay full time in France. Others like Anne and Michelle, who both reside in the States, but more than one thousand miles from their mothers' homes, could not, or would not, abandon their personal agendas because of caregiving complications associated with geographic inaccessibility. Who would blame them? There is no blame involved here. Not one of these women abandoned their responsibilities to supervise and coordinate care for their mothers and fathers. They did it long distance and at great personal cost to their health and peace of mind.

Just as in any other situation, the caregiving responsibilities grow over time. Only it is not difficult to imagine how stressful the job becomes when you are doing it from a distant location. There are the calls that interrupt your work or sleep to inform you that your mother has just been hospitalized and plans need to be made for her rehabilitation from, in one example, a transient stroke and fractured pelvis. Anne flew down to Florida to be with her mother and organize a plan for both rehab and her mother's ultimate disposition. The question arose: could Mom go home with care, or would she be receptive to an assisted living option and, in that case, would she be eligible for assisted living? As in most caregiving situations, nothing happens in neat linear progression. There are all kinds of irregularities and complications along the labyrinthine path, and for that Anne was prepared. But she was not prepared for the reaction of her brother who happened to be vacationing at the time with his family in Florida, but didn't want to have his vacation plans disrupted, in order to assist with his mother's planning. Mind you, he was not indifferent to his mother's condition; only he didn't see the need to upset his plans once she was out of the woods. One might think that this is not funny, but somehow Anne actually found some humor in her brother's slowness to understand. He was not being insensitive, merely dense. But in fairness, how many understand the rigors of caregiving unless they have experienced it firsthand?

This experience was only the first of many recalls to Florida for Anne. In the process, she was able to engage some ongoing care and emergency intervention for her mother. She, however, remained on high alert for the remainder of her mother's life and became a frequent flyer. All of which takes its toll.

As illustrated by Anne's experience with her brother, men often need to be socialized to the role of caregiver. Although social roles are changing, it is not unusual for men to delegate responsibilities and expect full cooperation. Women, who spend more time in the trenches, know that even the best home health aides need to be supervised and are more motivated when they experience the direct engagement of the family. Douglas, another reluctant brother, initially dismissed the importance of being directly engaged with his mother's aides but gradually came to realize the supportive function of his actual presence in his mother's home. This change in Douglas' behavior resulted primarily from his sister Susan's hectoring, but she was nonetheless grateful for his openness to adapt.

Paul, on the other hand, is an example of a man who served in the role of designated informal caregiver for both his parents. He is a single man in his sixties who had responsibility for his parents who lived across the country from him. He visited regularly and remained as long as necessary to resolve any unsettled issues. His primary focus initially was to make sure their finances were in order. He would joke about the fact that they thought they had much more money than they actually had and that their will included assets that were not in their possession. He wasn't as comfortable in areas related to personal care, but he made every effort to make sure that his parents had services . . . and could pay for them! It was no small achievement that he left his home on the Pacific coast to go to Florida on a regular basis despite his intolerance for the heat. No small sacrifice!

Paul does not have a sister. Therefore, the mantle of responsibility for his parents was bestowed upon him, and he graciously accepted his role. He did, however, join a caregiver support group, which surprised most of the people he knew. He was better known for his love of bass fishing than talking, but caregiving can bring out new aspects to our personalities, sometimes very admirably. It is fairly typical for expectations to be held of any single adult to fill a caregiving void for parents or even aunts, uncles or grandparents because of the assumption that the single adult has no family of her or his own and therefore more "free time."

No caregiver has to assume the role of caregiver for his or her parents or anyone for that matter; nor does a spouse have to fill that role for a husband or wife. As mentioned, it is the spouse who generally assumes the responsibility, regardless of status as husband or wife. Most families manage the needs of their aging relatives with grace and affection, not to mention perseverance. This does not mean that informal caregivers do not experience negative emotions such as depression, anger and frustration. Although most caregiving in this country is provided by family members, many families seek at least some formal support to help mitigate negative influences and better ensure the best possible arrangement for those in need.

FORMAL CAREGIVING

As already stated, most caregiving is provided informally. Although many families manage with part-time home care, many ultimately face the need to increase the hours as the person under care ages and loses functioning capacity. There are options for public financing of home care, which will be covered in Chapter 7, "Show me the Money."

Integrating outsiders into the home is no mean feat. Some dependent individuals accept assistance with grace and even appreciation. But even those most disposed toward receiving care will want the care to represent their own perception of need and desire. Benjamin found displeasure with caregivers who did not meet his personal qualifications for physical attractiveness. Since he was otherwise lucid, he could be convinced that he would need to be somewhat flexible. Sometimes the family is pleased with a caregiver, but not so the person receiving care, for any one of a number of seemingly (to the family) absurd reasons. There is no choice but to reach a compromise, and that often entails letting go of perfectly capable home health aides who don't meet your loved one's specifications. Yes, I believe, as much as possible, we need to satisfy the requests of the person under care. Sometimes, however, refusal of caregivers represents your loved one's need to maintain control and nothing more. If that is the case, as in the aforementioned case of Joan, a creative strategy is required and FAST! Dismissing aides can become a popular means of exercising authority and, consequently, the basis of a will struggle between parent and spouse, child or other. There are no easy answers to any of this. I can only say that, barring any major source of resistance, such as that associated with increasing dementia, generally, in the long run, your loved one will come around to some semblance of reasonability. To reiterate, there are peaks and valleys, ups and downs, throughout the caregiving process. How effectively issues are resolved has a lot to do with the fortitude and tolerance of the informal caregiver. But suffice it to say, one cannot expect an uninterrupted experience. In situations where the caregiving is not carefully monitored, one can expect upheaval. That is the primary source of informal caregiver burden. The question inevitably arises: "How can I take care of myself and also meet my commitments to my family member?" There is no one response to that question. Only, regardless of how one reconciles this challenge, the designated informal caregiver cannot ever escape the necessity of staying in charge of the situation when the dependent individual remains at home. Situations characterized by increasing mental deterioration represent an advanced caregiving challenge, which is addressed in Chapter 8.

Formal aides become one's best shot at maintaining some independence of your own as the child or spouse of the person under care.

PARADE OF AIDES

Many caregivers discuss the disruption created by the endless flow of home health aides. Lynn required help with managing her husband's needs following a stroke. She had part-time support but couldn't count on regular scheduling of personnel owing to one circumstance or another. Helene reiterated this same sentiment but reported that the agency with which she was affiliated did not even consider continuity in personnel in scheduling. You might think some of this has to do with source of payment and you wouldn't get this disruptive pattern in private pay situations. Rest assured, whatever the source of payment, you will experience disruptions. On the other hand, privately engaging an aide leaves one wide open to the pitfalls of no backup, or rather no backup for emergencies. Whether home care is privately or agency arranged, there are potential pitfalls.

In my experience, you "got to have luck" in finding the right fit for your loved one and you, but mostly you have to think smart. You have to think about what home care option you have selected and all the possible implications of your choice. I have known live-in aides, representing privately arranged and agency based/public and private payment arrangements, who lived for years with the person under their care with hardly any breaks. Breaks were factored into the plan and substitute care smoothly integrated. Many aides understand that they do not want live-in arrangements, and therefore there is self selection at the root of many a success story. Today, we are facing a shortage of home health aides, and that is problematic given the aging of the population—fewer personnel, less choice.

In general, most people interviewed reported appreciation for the support of home health aides in their lives. I think of the work of paid aides as nothing short of noble and self-sacrificing. I have come to love the people who have held my hand along the caregiving trail. I marvel at the phone calls I have gotten on aides' days off to check on my mother's status. This is more than a job to most of these women and men, who may serve in that role with less frequency but with no less sense of dedication. Caregiving is a spiritual undertaking, and I have taken many lessons from those who have entered my family's life in time of need. Without them, the option of remaining home for my mother, and many other people I know, would not have been possible.

It would be misleading not to mention that not every home health agency is managed effectively and efficiently. Another demanding function of being the DIC is monitoring for any issues associated with formal caregiving. Issues associated with inexperience or lack of proper training or unsuitability will arise and are likely to increase along with shortages in supply of home health personnel. Many problems seem to emerge from organizational lack of proper oversight and screening of personnel. Although it was unintentional, Sophia was thrown to the ground by an aide, unbeknownst to the agency, to have a seizure disorder. Other situations may arise from lack of oversight regarding Covid immunization. On the other hand, more than a fair share of reported problem situations were instigated by the one receiving care. There is the additional example of Thelma who threw a book at the aide because she seemed to be asleep, to include along with "throwing out the aide" or "calling the police." The DIC often needs to utilize every negotiation skill available and create new ones to manage conflicts and avoid the point of no return!

During the peak of the pandemic, bringing anyone into the home was a risk and still remains a risk despite increased vaccination rate. Public health monitoring is just another task that falls to the conscientious informal caregiver. And as we know, controversy abounds around vaccinations, compounding anxieties and creating tension.

Further, remaining at home is not necessarily the best option for every person in need of assistance or their families. Other options are explored in later chapters. Some options are not available or acceptable to all because of cost, cultural or other predilections that may dictate, for example, against residential placement in a nursing home. Despite general resistance to nursing home placement, if you live long enough, there is more than a slight chance that you will spend at least some time in rehabilitation. Therefore, the nursing home plays a central role for all of us in the continuum of care.

SPEAKING OF CONTINUUM OF CARE

The continuum of care or services represents all of the various agencies, organizations and even businesses that exist in the community to help support independent living. Communities known as NORCs or Naturally Occurring Retirement Communities develop in communities that disproportionately represent people over sixty. These communities take advantage of the disproportionate representation by offering more integrated and accessible services or conveniences to older people. NORCs can be a great boon to caregivers as well as older adults living independently. It is critical that caregivers establish an understanding of available resources to support their own efforts, including transportation services, respite services, meal delivery programs, not to mention "caregiver support groups" that are run under various agency and religious auspices. Area Agencies on Aging (AAA) are public or private non-profit agencies designated by the state to coordinate and offer services that help older adults remain in the home. Navigating the system efficiently can be extremely helpful in mitigating caregiver burden. Chapter 4 focuses on the subject of "Navigating the Medical System," which is an inherent aspect of caregiving regardless of whether home or residential based. Remaining chapters will take a close look at navigating residential options for caregiving, e.g., assisted living, life care communities and the dreaded nursing home.

CHAPTER 4

Navigating the Medical System

Just to set things straight from the outset, the United States does not have a medical system. We have a confusing arrangement of government and private financing, insurance, delivery and payment components that represent an alphabet soup of elements that attempt to meet the health needs of different target populations. Simply, this non-system was not designed, rather it was developed incrementally to fill holes in health-care delivery based predominantly on compromises among different special interest groups, i.e., the doctors' monopoly, business interests and, finally, consumer interests or community advocacy. Community advocacy did gain some momentum with the Affordable Health Care legislation but only on the basis of deep accommodation to the requirements of the insurance industry and amidst controversy from community groups on the far right, who fear that the United States is at the risk of turning "red," in the manner of the Bolsheviks, not the Republican Party.

So where does this leave you, the caregiver? Most people are at best confused and at worst finding themselves at the mercy of all those unwanted solicitors hawking different insurance products on your cell phone on a daily basis. I have become quite the expert at blocking calls.

Let's take the simplest scenario. The person under your care has Medicare, or Medicaid, depending upon financial status. Medicaid is needs based. Generally, those receiving Medicare have supplementary insurance that fills the gaps in Medicare coverage. I will get more into the financing later; however, for now, suffice it to say that, unless you join a managed care program or, under Medicaid, are forced to join a managed Medicaid program, you are "blessed" with the option of figuring out your own strategy for ensuring your health, rather than relying on your primary care provider (PCP) or managed care provider to refer you to another doctor. So here we deal primarily with the former situation.

In many cases, if not most, the person for whom you are caring has a primary physician. If you are lucky, that primary physician is a geriatrician, family practitioner or internist with a holistic perspective. There are not enough geriatricians to go around. The physician can be a great boon to the experience of a person receiving care but only up to a point. Chronic care management and very deliberate specialized intervention are the key to maintaining quality of life for older adults. On that note, it is important to recall that prevention and chronic care management have not been the principal modus operandi of medical care. In this country, medical treatment still vastly outpaces preventive care in medical practice. So caveat emptor! You must do your research.

Perhaps you are fortunate as I have been in locating just the right doctor for your loved ones. That's a good start, but don't take your eye off the road.

As an example, many years ago, my father, the sweetest, most gentle soul, who used his time to investigate every possible new technology at his disposal, decided on his own recognizance to try an experimental ablation procedure. If you don't know what that is, here's a brief description. This is a procedure that uses small burns or freezes to cause some scarring on the inside of the heart to help break up the electrical signals that cause irregular heartbeats. This can help the heart maintain a normal heart rhythm. His doctor, praise be, recommended a pacemaker at the time because of his advancing age and because it would have been a satisfactory, more conservative, less experimental-at-the-time option. My dad sought perfection, and he didn't want to be encumbered by the tried-and-true pacemaker. Who was I to argue? We scheduled the procedure. I accompanied him. Long story short, it didn't work. But "try, try, again!" Dad was invited to stay over at the hospital and repeat the procedure the next day. Well, we'd gone this far and so, "why not?"

Actually, why not? The second time around, the procedure did not work, but my dad had the satisfaction of contributing to medical science. He ultimately had a pacemaker implanted and lived very comfortably with it for many years to come.

There are many other instances of people getting procedures that, arguably, are unnecessary and invasive. Another example is Doris who went regularly for mammograms into her nineties. This was also a personal choice. Upon the discovery of a mass, she underwent treatment. The doctor wisely advised no further mammograms. There was the expectation that Doris would likely outlive any adverse outcome from any further complications. This same philosophy has guided the treatment of Randolph who at ninety-eight "probably" has progressing prostate cancer but is responding to hormone treatment satisfactorily. There is some question regarding a "blockage" that shows up on scans, but doctors, with consent of patient and family, have determined it best to avoid invasive procedures.

Sometimes doctors order tests to avoid liability, and many a caregiver and patient have mentioned suspicion about providers ordering tests and procedures to run up revenues because of financial imperatives. It is not great when patients suspect their physicians of malfeasance! Then there are those people who express frustration over not being able to get tests or pharmaceuticals because insurance doesn't cover the costs. It takes a delicate balance to maintain the right course of treatment, and the DIC must take on the role of arbiter in decision making. Sometimes, when the person is very old, you decide not to worry them with all the details. I think that is okay in many cases. As the health proxy, you need to be prepared for ethical challenges. If choices were easy, we would not have to consider ethical implications.

The point of all of this is that the first hurdle in managing the medical system is navigating the needs and desires of the one under your care, and that is no small feat.

Your loved one may resist going to the doctor or dentist, as in the case of Lydia who cancels her appointments just as quickly as her daughter can make them. Then begins the negotiation around motivating the recalcitrant relative. Sometimes it works. Other times, Lydia's daughter swallows her frustration and apologizes to the providers, who generally have been very understanding.

Conversely, there are those older adults who seem to spend most of their days going from one doctor to the next, and if you have one who is so inclined under your care and you are the designated driver, be prepared to spend a lot of time in doctors' offices.

But that is only the first of many challenges.

EMERGENCIES AT UNTIMELY HOURS

Anticipation of emergency needs is one of the hallmarks of life for the DIC. You never know when a mini crisis or something requiring intervention will hit, but likely, the timing will be terrible. Some of these "emergencies" are brought on by threats by formal caregivers to quit or, probably more often, demands by your loved one for you to immediately remove the caregiver from the home. These demands can be accompanied by threats to call 911 or actual calls. Other "emergencies" will generally arise when the DIC is taking some respite from supervisory responsibilities and the secondary informal caregiver (SIC) is overwhelmed by something that can be as significant as failure of the aide to show up or a "fall" or as insignificant as "mother is refusing to take her pills." None of this is really insignificant, but there are degrees of significance. They all become equally compelling when the DIC is "off duty." So you can expect a lot of phone calls, and sooner or later, you may be successful in "training" the secondary to provide protection without your involvement. Typically, there is a learning curve, and it takes a lot of management to achieve some kind of working solution.

The "major emergencies" warrant medical intervention. Unless in the rare instance you happen to be a medically trained professional, faced with an abnormality or injury of undecipherable significance, you are likely to call for emergency medical assistance. Frank had unsuccessful hip replacement, resulting in repeated dislocation, always at the oddest hours. His wife, as primary caregiver, would arrange for an ambulance to bring her husband (and herself) to the ER. The couple were well into their eighties at the time. Frank eventually needed corrective surgery by an alternate surgeon. The original surgeon had questionable competency, but unfortunately, his medical peers had done little to restrict his practice. I bring this up because doctors traditionally used the referral system as a deterrent against poor practice performance, but sometimes, in managed care situations, choices are restricted to doctors within the network, or patients are simply given a list of eligible specialists from which to self-select. In addition, utilization of referrals as a method to avert incompetency has its obvious limitations, and licensing boards have not been the quickest to impose sanctions. Thus, gatekeeping becomes the province of the already besieged caregiver. Managed care has many implications for medical practice, and those implications must be weighed against any financial or practical choices involved in insurance selection where choice is permitted. More to that point later.

The necessity to go to an ER has always been a daunting proposition, but with the ongoing pandemic, ER visits have taken on even more fearful and cumbersome dimensions. Lana and Spencer recently traveled two hours to get to an ER to visit their uncle and were not allowed in to see him. They had to deal with a messenger system that involved hand-written notes being passed to someone in the ER, who would eventually contact them with information. Understood—we are still dealing with an earthshaking event if not a pandemic, but that's just the point! Emergency rooms are overridden with patients, and personnel are understandably taxed beyond human capacity. Dr. Gabriel Bosslet, a pulmonologist from Indiana, recently stated (December 2021) that the one thing that can't be scaled up is personnel, and therefore, we experience gaps in management of emergencies along with spikes in Covid cases. Caregivers want to avoid ER visits for their loved ones unless the situation is desperate.

Nevertheless, injuries resulting from falls, chest pain, stroke, shortness of breath, complications from diabetes and other chronic illnesses are associated with greater frequency of ER use among the elderly. As in the case of Lana and Spencer's uncle, ER visits cannot be avoided.

The trick then is navigating admission to the hospital if necessary. In Uncle's case, it took almost forty-eight hours for a bed to become available. Often the patient is treated and sent home as in the case of Donald who suffers from Parkinson's as well as Crohn's disease and diabetes. He has been in the ER multiple times in a short span of time and has not been admitted. Instead, he has been going through a revolving door of ER treatment and release for months. Ellen, his wife, is providing much of his direct care as well as coordinating all aspects of his health care. Donald benefits from home-based therapy, which has its merit, particularly with the pandemic lingering, but Ellen could also use some respite. Ellen is a brick—emotionally strong and loyal—and she manages to maintain a positive outlook, but lately she has been wondering whether the couple has any option other than reliving a recurring nightmare week after week, "Ground Hog Day" gone amok.

HOSPITAL ADMISSIONS

In situations that clearly indicate the need for further medical assessment, patients generally are admitted to the hospital after what seems like an eternity. Patients over sixty-five frequently present at emergency rooms with agitation or confusion. Delirium is often under-recognized and often confused with irreversible dementia. Older patients with confusion or behavioral changes need to be assessed for underlying conditions and/or trauma. The issues usually compound upon admission unless diagnosed and treated. Naturally, the caregiver needs to keep an attentive eye on the situation to try to mitigate mental complications.

Frieda was admitted to a community hospital following a fall. Preliminary scans revealed a little fracture of unknown origin in her neck. The ER physician assistant tried to get Frieda to use a neck brace for reasons obvious to everyone but Frieda. She told the PA to wear it if he liked it. Once Frieda was admitted, the resistance persisted. The neck brace sat at the foot of the bed, a constant, thoroughly neglected, companion. The supervising physician sensibly succumbed to Frieda's wishes, with the understanding that he was hardly in a position to try to force a ninety-nine-year-old woman to follow his instructions. Frieda's daughter agreed that was a smart move. She had a lifetime of experience with her mother upon which to base this decision. Risk versus reward is a common theme in conflict resolution.

If there is anesthesia associated with the hospitalization, caregivers learn to be prepared for all kinds of generally reversible mental distortions. The experienced caregiver is not put off by the patient's confusion following surgery, which could amount to disorientation or memory loss. Debbie recalls her father's pattern of hallucinating after anesthesia. He experienced visitations from all kinds of wild life, particularly pigeons. He would suddenly warn her to move from where she was sitting because there were birds perched above her head. She would tell him he was only imagining these things, and they would have a good laugh about his "visualizations." But he still insisted that she take another seat, and she graciously would comply. Eventually these hallucinations ended. If they persist, they could be symptomatic of an underlying issue, such as psychosis or dementia.

Mental complications aside, admissions raise other very practical navigational issues.

THE THREE-DAY RULE

It is critical to be aware of THE RULE that requires the patient to have a medically necessary three-day consecutive inpatient hospital stay in order to be eligible for Medicare reimbursement for skilled nursing home rehabilitation. This rule had been waived during the pandemic, but it is important to keep abreast of the changes in status to avoid adverse financial consequences. Patients or health proxies can request hospital discharge planning evaluation from the quality information officer and ask about "safe discharge policy" and request a fast appeal no later than the day you are scheduled for discharge.

Hospitals are focused on the bottom line. Ethel, a woman of ninety-eight, was scheduled for immediate discharge without consultation with family. The family was told that she would be sent home the very same day when no preparations for her care were in place. Finally, the case manager was able to negotiate a twenty-four-hour postponement in order for home health to be coordinated. That night a storm of almost hurricane proportions hit, and yet there was no modification of discharge plan, although no one could get to the hospital or to Ethel's home because of transportation breakdown. It took some further negotiating before Ethel was allowed to stay another day. So be prepared to be an advocate for your loved one, as "snapping people back to reality" may be a further negotiating skill you need to have in your armamentarium.

You may recall the situation of Anne and her brother from Chapter 2 in which the brother had to be encouraged to assist with the mother's discharge planning as he was on vacation. Sometime after her return home, Anne's mother suffered another brief stroke that landed her back in the hospital. Anne was notified and immediately flew to her mother's side, only to discover the hospital had already arranged transfer to a nursing home without consideration of the three-day rule. They had gotten approval from her mother's husband who knew nothing about the rule. This time Anne's brother, conveniently, an attorney stepped, if not jumped, into the breach. Brother and sister were able to negotiate a compromise on the billing after much argumentation.

The three-day rule for SNF (skilled nursing facility) admission had been suspended during the pandemic, but the rules change and it is important to keep abreast of any new developments. It is equally important to know that Medicare will only reimburse for 100 days in a benefit period for those patients who meet Medicare requirements (skilled rehabilitative therapies), and therefore if your loved one is not eligible, the stay will not be reimbursed. So it is better to err on the side of caution and be aware of the financial implications of nursing home admission.

MANAGED CARE

Managed care options vary depending upon the insurer and the delivery system. Choices exist for many people and vary from state to state. The subject at issue here is whether enrollment in a managed care program is beneficial, and the response is a definitive "it depends." However, one program that I have found personally satisfactory in my caregiving role is PACE, Program of All-Inclusive Care for the Elderly. I discovered PACE serendipitously in assisting a member of my family in coordinating home care. You may have discovered the difference between a CHHA (certified home health agency) and a LHCSA (licensed health care service agency), but if not, the former is allowed to bill Medicare and the latter can only work with Medicaid, private insurance and private pay. We will explore payment options in greater depth in Chapter 7.

It was the licensed nurse who, in evaluating my relative for long-term care eligibility, alerted me to the existence of PACE. These programs provide comprehensive home care and social services to community-dwelling elderly individuals, most of whom are dually eligible for Medicare and Medicaid benefits. One statement jogged my interest, and it will forever remain at the forefront of my awareness. She said, "PACE, in this case, ARCHCARE PACE, keeps people out of nursing homes." And her words have proven prophetic. This was before I knew what I know now. I consider these words among the most propitious in my experience as a gerontologist and caregiver. I mention this now because this managed care organization, ARCHCARE, had made it possible for me to keep my own loved one at home. The program has many aspects. House calls (remember those?) from doctors and nurses and transportation have been a godsend. Participants also are not subject to the three-day rule, and the program offers some respite services. Although this program is not for everyone, because there are certain restrictions, I offer this testimony as evidence of how challenging it can be to search out the best option for managing your requirements. Sometimes you can thank "dumb luck."

As a DIC, it is incumbent upon one to explore the best possible available delivery system to meet respective caregiving needs. Betty Davis is oft quoted as saying, "Aging ain't for sissies," and I would add, "Nor is caregiving for sissies." It's a lot of work with a lot of reward, and sometimes one uncovers a rare find, as I did in my search for help for my loved one.

You have probably already discovered there is a wide range of managed care models representing another alphabet soup of options.

Chances are, if you have a health plan, you will encounter some features of managed care. The general rule of thumb is, the more restrictive your choices are, the lower will be your cost. Ironically, my experience with ARCHCARE PACE has demonstrated that comprehensive care can compensate for limited self-selection. These are individual decisions that require informed scrutiny. This is not to suggest that the route I chose for my relative has been without its difficulties, but the trip has been better and a mite easier than it could have been.

Many different models of health delivery have cropped up over the years to provide order to the chaos that represents the continuum of care in the United States. The aforementioned NORCs represent one example of American ingenuity in pulling together an array of supplementary services and activities designed to help maintain the elderly in the community. After all, man or woman does not live by medical care alone. NORC programs, funded jointly by government agencies and private organizations, constitute a middle ground between independent living and long-term care for the elderly. Other private alternatives have also developed to fill this void.

Americans are very creative, and in the next chapter, "Moving On Out," we will take a closer look at the private communities that have emerged to offer coherent care for some who can afford the price of admission and who are able and willing to leave their homes.

CHAPTER 5

Moving On Out

There are those individuals and couples who, in the interest of being proactive, and sometimes in the interest of not becoming a burden to their children, come to the decision to seek an assisted living facility as their needs begin to grow. This group, by the way, represents just 2 percent of the older adult population. One might be tempted to view those who make this decision to assume the mantle of caregiver for themselves as being very independent "captains of their destiny." In most cases, the choice to move to a residential community is really more a matter of personal preference or family pressure and financial feasibility than anything else. As a potential or practicing caregiver, you may experience a great deal of satisfaction in knowing that those family members for whom you bear responsibility are getting regular meals, hospitality services, have social connections and may even have the additional option of transitioning through different levels of care, including memory care or skilled nursing. Once again, it is important to keep your eye on the ball. Also, let us not forget that assisted living generally comes with a high price tag.

One's role as the designated informal caregiver does not terminate upon the admission of your parents, let's say, to an independent living or assisted living facility. It just changes.

COST OF CARE

First and foremost, one faces the need to scrutinize the cost breakdown of assisted living in any form. By this time, most people are aware that it is important to study the financials of Continuing-Care Retirement Communities before signing on. Continuing-Care Retirement Communities or Life Care (Plan) Communities, as you probably already know, are multi-level facilities that offer the appropriate level of care across a continuum. I had a chance to observe firsthand the life cycle of one particular community through the experience of a close friend of my family. June joined a life care community and remained in the assisted living component for about ten years until her death in 2018. At first it was great, and a lot of that had to do with the fact that June knew a lot of women who also resided there. She played bridge, enjoyed concerts, went on "shopping" excursions. It was all it was cracked up to be. When June suffered a broken pelvis, she was able to stay in the skilled nursing facility that was part of the continuum of care. Noteworthy was the quality of the food as evidenced by the number of visitors who enjoyed sharing a meal with June for a reasonable fee. It was after a few years that June started to say that the meal quality was not the same as when she first arrived. Well, you didn't have to be Miss Marple to decipher that the organization had initiated cost-cutting measures that were most recognizable to June and others in the form of their daily bread.

June was not someone to complain arbitrarily. But a little investigating revealed that the retirement community had a lot of vacancies and was strapped financially. A number of June's friends had passed away, and there were no new recruits to fill the void. You also don't have to be an actuary to understand that, since the contracts in this community guaranteed a return of six-figure initial buy-in payment, the financial situation was dire. Therefore, from the standpoint of quality of life, not only did June have fewer friends in her age group, but she also experienced adverse consequences associated with deteriorating food quality and staff shortages. She voluntarily carried on under reduced circumstances until her passing, although her children offered her the option of living with them. The children then discovered the full impact of the community's insolvency when seeking the guaranteed refundable entry fee. There is no mystery here as the situation ultimately was resolved but only after many months of legal negotiation.

Cash-deficient communities raise questions about what is being done with entrance fees, as pointed out by Peter Finch in a recent article, "7 Ways to Judge a Retirement Community's Financial Health" (*New York Times*, March 9, 2018). In other words, do your homework. Properly evaluated for financial soundness and quality of services, Life Care (Plan) or Continuing-Care Communities can, however, provide peace of mind and continuing security for members. As an example, Kate moved from the Midwest to a life care community in New Jersey because her sister was a resident there, and her daughter lived on the East Coast and could visit more regularly. The adjustment was not easy, but Kate, a stalwart Midwesterner, persevered and was able to settle into a very comfortable routine. Similarly, Edith chose a continuing-care community that offered just the right balance between independent living and access to on-site health care support, including skilled nursing. Edith, who is known for a sense of humor, realized that she missed some of the fine print when she signed the contract. She and a friend reread the contract and discovered that the community had the right to send her to an alternative nursing home if there was no availability in the on-site facility, or seemingly for almost any other reason. Instead of panicking, true to form, Edith sardonically responded that she had better stay well or she might wind up in East Jabip or Outer Mongolia. However, she still had her attorney follow up for clarification.

You might also want to make sure you read the exit options of the contract so you know what to expect if you decide to move and you have paid a high entry fee. Different contracts offer different options for payment and refunds upon resale of the unit. Often families must wait months for any refund, and so it is good to be prepared for the fact that the refundable sum may not immediately be used to pay for a new facility in case of a move, even in the best of circumstances.

Assisted living also comes with its share of surprises. Assisted living is the next rung on the ladder for many people who start out in an independent or senior living community that offers certain services such as meals and dining, scheduled social activities and transportation to appointments. Assisted living is designed for those who have varying levels of personal or medical care needs, and in some ways, this arrangement liberates families from having to provide support to older adults with health or functional needs.

Jeanette moved with her husband, who had Alzheimer's disease, to an independent living community with the support of some home care provided through the Veterans Administration. She managed with part-time assistance until his death and then stayed on as a single resident. In typical fashion, as Jeanette grew older, she experienced growth in her needs. At that point, her son arranged for her to transition to an assisted living facility that represented the next level of service. Assisted living was more costly but not unaffordable for Jeanette. That arrangement worked until Jeanette suffered a broken hip from a fall. After hospitalization, she went to a nursing home for a period of time for rehabilitation. She and her son planned on her returning to the assisted living community only to be met with resistance from the facility because Jeanette was now wheelchair bound. Not every assisted living restricts the use of a wheelchair, but it can happen.

Even when the assisted living offers services to support residents with infirmities, who, for example, may be wheelchair bound or suffer from memory loss or other challenges in performing activities of daily living, support comes with a price. Charlotte and Tom, whom you might remember from a preceding chapter as having taken an impulsive leap in furtively registering for an assisted living community, weren't really prepared for the realities of their new lifestyle or the costs. After a very brief honeymoon, they realized that Charlotte's daughter had been right in cautioning them to take a first-floor unit. Had they waited, one would have become available, but in their haste, and in the spirit of independence, they took the only unit available on an upper floor. With both of them experiencing ambulatory issues, getting to the dining room became a burden. They started to order room service for a couple of their meals and then were shocked by the additional charges. They were equally shocked by the additional cost of medication management and routine security checks on their well-being. They could afford these added expenses, but as depression era alumni, they found the situation perturbing, to say the least. Naturally, their dissatisfaction was levelled at Janet for not warning them. Janet, for her part, was more concerned about maintaining medical care for her mother. The assisted living offered on-site nurse practitioner visits (for a fee) and subsequent physician referral as appropriate. This satisfied Janet's principal concerns but did not serve in any way to assuage her mother's concerns about the costs.

My father used to tell a joke. Actually, he loved to tell jokes and, frankly, I didn't really have patience for them, but one stands out. It describes the experience of a man who gets a peek at the afterlife before his actual demise and he sees the kingdom of heaven in all its glory. When he passes and literally passes through what he thinks are the heavenly gates, he encounters a completely different scene straight out of Rodin's Gates of Hell. He calls for Saint Peter and demands an explanation, to which Saint Peter simply responds, "The last time you came here you were a tourist; now you are a resident!"

Of course, this is a gross exaggeration designed to make a point. Check it all out, or conversely, you can always check yourself out. Only moves can be very traumatic. Unless you really have a lot of energy (and money) to spend on relocation, you might want to take a lesson from Charlotte and Tom. As illustrated, however, the older adults under your care are not necessarily going to listen to their informal caregiver's advice.

Recall the example of Bernice and William from Chapter 2, who failed to make any plans for their continuity of care despite William's compounding physical challenges. Ginny tried desperately to encourage them to consider a life care community that would have provided a safety net for William in offering skilled nursing as part of the package. They would not hear of it even though the family accountant also encouraged consideration of a very desirable community very close to their home. Even after William's sister moved to a life care community, the couple remained adamantly opposed to any such move.

Some people are more compliant and even eager to make a change to assisted living or a life care community. This inclination generally comes along with the growing realization of the need for additional services, and since most of the assisted living population consists of women over the age of eighty-five, the move likely is associated with the loss of one's spouse. Whereas the average age of senior living residents is 84, the average age of assisted living residents is 86.9 years, and women represent 75 percent of the assisted living population. Of course, the average doesn't tell you the mode or the age that appears most often, but clearly, people in assisted living are older than people in independent living communities.

As already stated, there is a certain liberation from certain caregiving responsibilities for the family members of older people residing in assisted living communities, but the need to maintain oversight never diminishes. Ultimately it is the DIC who will take the greatest pains in ensuring medical follow-up or medication review. These actions don't necessarily take place automatically, and sometimes delays in scheduling visits with specialists may have serious consequences, such as in the case of Charlotte whose mini strokes led to a heart attack. In some ways, assisted living facilities are serving as nursing homes despite not being adequately staffed or resourced to offer full protection to residents. The designated informal caregiver is a critical asset in ensuring safeguards.

I am a firm believer in risk versus reward trade-offs. Assisted living options are excellent alternatives to nursing homes for many who might otherwise have no choice. The offering of health services is a great blessing to people who need support in maintaining their independence. Perhaps in an aging society, we can look at these facilities as residential alternatives to the traditional alternative of nursing "homes." For those who can afford them, they may be just the answer as long as you ask the right questions and, as the designated informal caregiver, maintain close surveillance of your loved one's activities while allowing for some exposure to risk.

This need to balance risk versus reward is a hallmark of caregiving regardless of the venue. Designated caregivers for stay-at-home family members remark on the fact that they feel they are running an assisted living facility, albeit on a micro level. The coordination of services is constant. Ensuring the safety of your loved one can become an obsession, with many families relying on cameras to monitor for security and personal safety. "I fell and I can't get up" is a well-known admonition to hook your loved one up to a medical alert or life line. Of course, Bernice, not atypically, used her pendant as window dressing until a camera was substituted, placing increased responsibility upon Ginny to maintain constant surveillance when Bernice was alone. The final straw came when Ginny, who happened to be out of town, "checked in" with her mother only to discover that Bernice was not in her bed at 12:00 a.m. She panned the room and no sign of mother, until alas, she saw a finger wagging at the far reaches of the camera's lens. After frantic calls to her brother and a neighbor, who had agreed to keep the keys, Mother was discovered, alert but prostrate, on the floor where she said she "sat down." Upon arrival of EMS, it was determined that all was well for the moment. However, as a result of that escapade, Bernice was inflicted with full time coverage that, previously, she had resisted. Only when threatened with the need to move did Bernice reluctantly agree to the recruitment of an overnight aide, whom she fondly referred to as the Night Watchman.

I mention this because, of course, there is much value to the caregiver in knowing that one's charge is safe and sound. It is unlikely that your loved ones will admit to the need for "babysitting." It is more likely that those in your care will fend off any efforts to upset the status quo. A good friend of Bernice's, Martha, shared the same enthusiasm for night-time excursions. At the tender age of 100, she decided to get something she desperately needed off the top shelf of her closet. She didn't make it up the ladder, fortunately, having fallen and broken an arm before she reached any treacherous height. Thankfully, this happened in the early morning, and Martha was discovered fairly quickly by her regular aide upon her arrival. Happily, this encounter did not interfere with Martha's hairdresser's appointment that week.

Another contributing caregiver reports that her mother, who had a full-time aide, would insist upon maintaining her night-time routine of cleaning, when she was having trouble sleeping, and this habit persisted even after Rhoda (along with her aide) entered an assisted living facility. Some facilities allow you to have your own private aide. The very accommodating aide would also accompany Rhoda on her cleaning "jobs" even once they had relocated to a facility. These examples clearly illustrate the need for close observation. Close brushes with disaster often provide the incentive for increasing formal caregiving or seeking assisted living.

As stated, assisted living can be a great boon to the caregiver if—a big if—affordable and a negotiable option—another big if. Martha refused to move to a senior residence and could not afford additional hours. Fortunately, she was capable of being extremely reasonable and agreed to refrain from anymore night-time jaunts.

BOARD AND CARE (ADULT) HOMES

There is another less commonly known long-term care living option that sits somewhere between assisted living and a skilled nursing facility along the care continuum. These are small homes in residential neighborhoods, equipped and staffed to care for a small number of residents. They don't provide skilled nursing. They generally are less expensive than assisted living facilities and certainly less expensive than skilled nursing facilities. When Jeannette was refused reentry to her assisted living residence, her son was directed to a board and care home that accepted her, although she was not weight bearing. Even as Jeanette's cognitive function deteriorated, perhaps as a function of her increasing depression, the board and care facility continued to provide service and filled an important gap in the continuum of care for Jeanette and her persevering son. Board and care was also the answer for Constance who, after entering an assisted living facility and while awaiting hip replacement surgery, suffered a heart attack that resulted in a brief hospitalization, along with her involuntary discharge from the assisted living facility and ultimate transition to a board and care home. You never know where hope lies or what's out there until you have a pressing need.

This points to the caregiver's need to continually reinvent the care plan. Nothing remains static, and that is perhaps what makes the task of being a caregiver so formidable. Assisted living may serve some individuals for the duration of their lives, but with increased longevity and inevitable age-related losses, it is very likely that assisted living may not be the definitive solution to the caregiving quandary. Thus, we have seen the emergence of the life or continuing care community as a more comprehensive model of care.

Most assisted living facilities offer physical, occupational or speech therapy (71.4 percent), hospice (67.7 percent) and skilled nursing (66.1 percent). But let us not forget that only approximately 2 percent (of the older adult population) currently live in assisted living facilities, while about 5 percent of adults older than sixty-five live in nursing homes with 50 percent of the latter population being eighty-five years or older. To reiterate, most people in this country stay at home until, if and when, managing care at home becomes too unwieldy a task for even the most determined older care recipient and persistent and persevering designated informal caregiver. I think one of the positives of continuing care community life is that the nursing home is an integrated aspect of the community and may supplement rather than replace one's home in the residential part of the community. Residents can move back and forth between levels of service if necessary. If Bernice and William had moved together, even if William needed extended skilled care, they would have been on the same campus.

But then, "what if" only leads us down the path to second guessing and lost opportunity. Bernice would never have had a home of her own if the couple had gone the practical route and moved to a life care community, and so, once again, the situation boils down to measuring risk versus reward and learning to live with ambiguity. Most of all as a caregiver, it is best to learn to embrace uncertainty but only after reading the fine print in the contract.

Placement in an extended care skilled nursing facility often occurs only after every other caregiving option has been exhausted. The following Chapter 6 focuses on the trials, tribulations and glory of life in an SNF (Skilled Nursing Facility), with tribute to all involved in what often constitutes the final leg of the caregiving journey.

CHAPTER 6

Navigating the Nursing Home

The day of reckoning may come crashing like a thunderbolt or, conversely, may creep up on "little cat feet." Fifty percent of the population over sixty-five will spend some time in a skilled nursing facility in their lifetime. Often this stay is for short-term rehab, and sometimes, nursing homes become the primary residence for older adults. In fact, approximately 40 percent of the long-term residents of nursing homes are over the age of eighty-five. Although the majority of adults with dementia live at home, more than 50 percent of residents in assisted living and nursing homes have some form of dementia. It is safe to say that there is a good chance that you and your loved one will see the inside of a nursing home at some point in the caregiving life cycle.

THE SHORT-TERM STAY

Many skilled nursing stays follow on the heels of a hospital-ization. Be reminded of the three-day rule explained in Chapter 4. If your loved one meets the criteria for skilled nursing and/or therapy care, Medicare will cover limited stays in a skilled nursing facility (SNF) or rehabilitation facility.

William met the criteria for Medicare reimbursement and spent a number of short stays in a nursing home before his even-tual permanent relocation to an extended care facility. These stays would follow a typical pattern of initial acquiescence to the reality of the situation, followed soon after by persistent insistence upon being liberated from the bondage to which he felt he was being sub-jected. Ginny and her brother were able to calm William's fears of permanent abandonment and appeal to his better instincts on most occasions. William would grudgingly accept his need for physical therapy and would put in his time with the understanding that he would eventually be returning home. William was a very reason-able man in many ways. He was able to utilize his therapy to the utmost advantage.

Not so Benjamin. Benjamin needed skilled nursing and rehabilitation following an emergency admission for serious com-plications resulting from urologic disease and prostate problems. His niece found him in his apartment on the floor when he didn't respond to her phone calls. To his credit and typical of the valiance of his, the "greatest generation," his only comment was, "What took you so long?" In the ER he experienced heart block and narrowly escaped cardiac arrest. However, in Benjamin's mind, he was fit as a fiddle and ready to leave the hospital almost as soon as he was placed in a bed.

The real trouble, however, started upon his eventual move to the skilled nursing component of the medical center. From the moment of his arrival, he began his refrain of "Get me out of here!" His niece was caught between a rock and a hard place and tried to cajole him into some attitude of compliance. The hospital staff continually called her with requests for clothing, food and visitation and, while juggling her full-time work and the nursing home's geographic inaccessibility with her uncle's need for support and resources, managed somehow to provide whatever help she could. Her acts of diligence were usually rewarded with her uncle's accusations of failure to get him released from the nursing home. When the time finally arrived for discharge, Benjamin made his own plans for home care. He canvassed the community for assistance and identified an individual who was willing to provide care, through his own efforts and those of his kith and kin. Alice, his niece, tried to warn Benjamin against moving ahead with this plan, as he was being sent home with a catheter and couldn't walk independently, let alone take care of any of his basic needs. She tried desperately to convince him to accept help from professionals, as in, certified home health aides. He insisted that she was over-controlling and overly pessimistic.

Long story short, Benjamin and friends' plan imploded within approximately forty-eight hours. Benjamin had to be readmitted to the hospital under emergency conditions. He felt no responsibility for his choices, but instead asked Alice, "How could you have let me go home with those people?" During the course of the hospitalization, doctors determined that medication was not the answer to Benjamin's irregular heart beat and that he needed a pacemaker. After successful implantation of the pacemaker, Benjamin faced another sojourn in a skilled nursing facility. Looking back, Alice can recall this next phase with some degree of amusement, but at the time, she could only wonder whether the stress she was experiencing would catapult her into an adjoining room to the one occupied by her dear uncle.

Benjamin went on a hunger strike and refused to eat anything but "the chocolate drink," otherwise known as Ensure. He also refused physical therapy and any other therapy being offered. To cut to the chase, eventually and happily, Benjamin survived his own worst instincts and returned home with qualified support from a licensed home health agency. Once back in his own residence, and restored to his position of lord of the manor, he adjusted very well to the care that afforded him his freedom to be at home. The lesson from this is that short stays in a nursing home can be very demanding for the designated informal caregiver as well as the individual under her care. Also, those under care very often stretch the limits of your patience and resist what you think is their best interest, but if Benjamin and William serve as examples, they often surprise you with their resilience and capacity for survival.

WHO RESIDES IN A SKILLED NURSING HOME?

Before looking at some nursing home caregiving experiences, let's take a glance at those who represent the permanent population of these establishments. As already stated, the oldest of the old constitute the majority of residents. Most of the residents are women, and a majority suffer from dementia and/or some mental disorder. The under-sixty-five population with serious mental illness continues to grow. The most common reason that older people live in nursing homes is some type of disability when it comes to performing the activities of daily living. The most common reason aging parents are admitted into a nursing home is severe cognitive and/or physical decline that requires them to need twenty-four-hour care. Nursing homes can be described as the caregiving option of last resort. However, because nursing homes generally accept Medicaid, they are also often the only affordable option for older adults with multiple physical and mental challenges.

Many designated informal caregivers mention that a parent went to a nursing home when it no longer was possible to meet their needs at home. Many people do not know about community Medicaid, and other families may not have the resources to supplement the formal care. Also, home health care workers are at a premium today, and shortages are likely to get worse. On the other hand, the pandemic has placed more pressure on families to keep relatives out of nursing homes because of fear of exposure to the disease. Still, for many, there is no alternative to residential care in an extended care facility. Most people report mixed opinions about the quality of care in nursing homes, but at least today we can rely on government regulation to better ensure a certain level of standardized care. There are even some smaller nursing homes that are cropping up to provide a more comfortable and accommodating space for residents. Of course, with many residents being deeply physically or mentally challenged, residential amenities may be less significant than the quality of direct care.

In checking out assisted living residences and nursing homes, I have often felt that the prettier ones are designed to appeal to the family members more than the residents. I remember visiting an Alzheimer's wing of a nursing home that reminded me of a first-class hotel, and I thought to myself how irrelevant that is to the person with advanced dementia. I can't say it didn't make me happy to be in such splendid surroundings. I wouldn't rule it out for being too attractive. In my travels through nursing homes, I have learned to appreciate the need to make family members comfortable to encourage them to visit. So even if the spouse or child of the resident seems to be enjoying the activities, such as the sing-a-longs or religious services, holiday parties and crafts more than the resident, they are enjoying each other's interaction around a common pursuit. That is a good thing. With more staffing, I would like to see an expansion in small support groups for residents as well as family members, especially now with people living longer and the demand for nursing homes likely to grow. Unfortunately, many nursing homes are experiencing shortages of nurses and aides at this time. However, still, many nursing homes try to surpass people's expectations and provide as homelike and companionable an experience as possible for those residents with the capacity to mutually engage. Not all upgrades are for the better, however. I witnessed one example of supposed progress in the closing of an imposing building, what you'd call an "old pile," and opening of a shiny new structure that filled me with some regret. The new structure seemed sterile, without the warmth of the traditional living rooms or communal dining rooms with linen table cloths. Instead, residents were confined to tables set up in the unit in which they resided for their meals. No more congregate meals in a dining room designed for that purpose. Perhaps this new manner of food preparation and delivery is more cost efficient and more hygienic but, without a doubt, less social and less formal. Call me old fashioned, but this change reflected a culture shift that, arguably, was not an improvement.

I can see things getting worse before they get better with more people requiring services and increasing limitations on resources; however, on a slightly upbeat note, my experience as a camp director for a non-profit organization taught me that creative programming can be cost effective. I know I digress. However, I try to keep positive, and I have seen much that leaves room for optimism in nursing home environments and some things that can be improved without necessarily increasing costs. So the lesson here is to check out the institution carefully and not be influenced solely by first impressions.

TALES FROM THE NURSING HOME

Many residents in nursing homes suffer from cognitive dysfunction. Marilyn, Cynthia's mother, was admitted for extended care after falling and breaking her leg. Marilyn suffered from advancing dementia, and her doctor basically told Cynthia, "It is time." She had been living with Cynthia's sister, but despite the heroic efforts of family members, Marilyn's needs were no longer manageable at home. Cynthia admits that the transition to an extended care facility was simplified by her mother's disorientation and loss of attachment to her own home. This made the move easier all around and serves as a good example of how these moves typically unfold for many people. Once "inside," Marilyn's family visited her almost every day. Cynthia felt that it was critical for the family to provide oversight for her mother. That sentiment is shared by many family members.

Anne expressed exactly the same viewpoint with regard to her mother's intermittent nursing home visits. She was reminded of the time that her mother had been admitted to the nursing home after a car accident and, being in pain, expressed the need for some medication. Anne went down the hall to request the nurse's attention (pre-Covid) and was strictly told to return to her mother's room and wait for said nurse to complete her vitamin dispensing activity. Anne dutifully followed orders and waited while her mother winced in pain. According to Anne, on the occasion of her next visit, she brought some BENGAY for her mother to help with the back pain. The nurse witnessed what Anne did not realize was a major transgression and threatened her with permanent expulsion from the nursing home for bringing an unprescribed liniment across its threshold.

Not all nursing homes, nurses or aides are equal! The point is that vigilance is always the best caregiver practice. And, of course, that takes its toll. One of the major areas of watch keeping in a nursing home relates to the laundry. It is common practice in nursing homes to put labels in residents' clothing. It is also common practice for clothing to go missing, and many caregivers report clothing crises. For instance, there's the crisis of new clothes that go missing. Doreen learned the hard way that sometimes protocols for protecting clothing are not efficiently enforced. Because her mother's clothes were not provided with labels on the day of her arrival, they managed to find their way to somewhere other than the closet in which Doreen had left them. After that, Doreen decided to take matters into her own hands and took her mother's clothes to the subterranean depths in which she discovered the "man responsible for putting labels in clothes." She did get a dressing down from him for trespassing. She unwittingly had entered the floor that housed certain unmentionable services. Use your imagination! But she got the job done, as well as a lesson in digital label design from the same individual who had "caught her in the act."

William moved into the nursing home accompanied by some good quality sweaters. Instructions were given to aides not to put the sweaters in with the machine wash. They not only went in with the machine wash (and dryer), what emerged were miniature versions of their original selves, suitable as nice attire for Ken, as you may recall, Barbie's boyfriend. Ok, Ginny and her mom initially found this disturbing, but somewhat amusing, and learned the hard way not to bring anything of value into the nursing home. They also learned that any unsolicited requests for special consideration of personal items would generally go unheeded. As long as William was receiving adequate care, they could live with it. You choose your battles. You learn to anticipate lost merchandise and not leave items of value in your loved one's possession. Protecting possessions is not staff's first priority.

Benjamin's glasses went missing for a while because they were removed from his face in the hospital and did not follow him to his nursing home bed. Same for Estelle's teeth. It took a great deal of detective work for their relatives to track down these items and receive the proper authorization to have them released to their custody. Oh, yes, there are many rules to observe in nursing homes as well as hospitals. Make sure you are an authorized personal representative.

But the need for the caregiver to maintain vigilance extends beyond the protection of property. For instance, your loved one may need protection from another combative resident. Doreen's mother was assigned a room with an aggressive patient, and she had to advocate to get her mother moved to another room. Similarly, Carl was depressed, and his son thought it might have something to do with the fact that his dad's roommate, who had a very poor prognosis, was hooked up to a ventilator in the next bed. His dad subsequently was assigned a single room but not until after Carl had "argued his case" with the executive director whose preliminary response was to recommend that Carl take his father home. Carl had no means of caring for his debilitated dad, and when the head nurse heard about this "recommendation," she was extremely distressed. Carl felt validated by the head nurse and reported overall satisfaction with his dad's treatment in the nursing home, but he reiterated the need to maintain a close watch.

The need to be vigilant regarding "loss" has even more intriguing implications. Sometimes the missing target is the resident herself.

I was first made aware of the high incidence of "wandering" that goes on and the precautions taken against elopement when I got on an elevator with a very lovely lady and an alarm went off. The elevator door did not close. I wondered what was going on until I noticed the tracking bracelet on the resident's wrist. I discovered that nursing homes take various precautions to prevent wandering and possible harm to mentally compromised residents. Most of the time these precautions are effective.

At least one resident, however, managed to fly under the radar. Elizabeth's aunt Susan had a history of "running" before she entered the nursing home. Old habits die hard, and she somehow managed to get out, only to be discovered, by means of a tracking device, at the railroad station. In her younger years, she would regularly take the train to visit her grandmother, and that was what she was planning to do. Yes, there is a sweetness to Aunt Susan's initiative, and Elizabeth recounts the episode with deep fondness and glee.

In recent years, nursing homes have made efforts to afford challenged individuals as much freedom as possible. Some even encourage dating. Philip recalls his mother's association with a male resident that basically amounted to them sitting together side by side in their wheelchairs throughout much of the day. Philip's mother had advanced Alzheimer's and thought the gentleman next to her was her deceased husband. The gentleman, content with the arrangement, offered no resistance. On some level, they had a connection. Karen relates her experience with her mentally compromised aunt Sonya and her aunt's roommate, a woman with all her faculties, who took great joy each day in helping Sonya get dressed and out for the day's activities. The two women stayed together as much as possible in appreciation of one another's company. There are some lovely relationships that form in extended care facilities.

Respect for residents' rights is a principal standard of care in nursing homes today, and that comes with some risk attached that, in my estimation, is generally worth the reward.

NOW, RESIDENT

Getting back to the daily life of a nursing home resident, the experience plays out in different ways. For more highly functional residents, of course, there are group activities and also opportunities for solo activity, such as use of computers or fitness workouts. For those who enter for post-acute care but whose status converts to long-term care, a pattern emerges that is inherently problematic.

William ultimately needed too much care to be managed at home. After what turned out to be his final hospital admission and transfer for rehabilitation, he made the decision to remain in the nursing home. In accounting for his complete change in attitude, his daughter Ginny suggested that he was getting bored at home and this nursing home seemed very inviting to him at the time. His wife Bernice was determined to bring him back home despite the impracticality. She had promised him that she would never leave him in a nursing home. It was a very nice nursing home, according to Ginny, but her concern was that William came to this decision riding the high of his new situation, without realizing he was in a honeymoon phase. For a while, the change seemed to rejuvenate William's spirits. He had his hair dyed to its original color, something which came as a bit of a shock to his family. He was receiving multiple types of therapy, paid for by Medicare, and would continue to do so for some time until he reached the limit for Medicare reimbursement for skilled nursing and therapy. Ginny and her brother had a sense that the honeymoon wouldn't last, but the decision had been made and application for long-term care under Medicaid had been filed.

William remained committed to the plan until after a period of time, despite daily visits from his wife and at least one of his children, he became determined to go home. Ginny would like to say that this resolved to everyone's satisfaction, but that was not the case. William, caught in a downward spiral of frailty, could not return to the home that had not been modified to meet his growing needs, without severe risk to himself and also his wife's capacity for endurance. Ginny's brother observed that the decline in William's mental health accompanied the decline in his daily rehabilitation services, begging the question of what's wrong with a system that does not foster ongoing rehabilitation for nursing home residents. The simple answer to that question is "Show me the money," which happens to be the title of the next chapter. If you want supplementary rehab after you have exhausted your benefits, you can pay out of pocket if you can so afford.

FINAL THOUGHTS

We are getting older as a society, and the resources are limited. The pandemic woke us up a little to the need to be cognizant of public health concerns, but we have a long way to go and money is tight. All things considered, I came away from the nursing homes I visited with deep gratitude for the people who provide the care, including the designated informal caregivers who, through the strength of familial bonds, demonstrate their dogged determination to care for their elders, often at deep personal sacrifice.

CHAPTER 7

Show Me the Money: Paying For It

In observing the lengths to which people today must go to ensure that they have the means to support their care throughout an increasingly longer life span, I am constantly reminded of how people used to manage. They had more children. They still do in poor countries. One of the reasons for having more children was (and still is) the need for adequate resources in one's old age to support increasing demand for care. No, I am not promoting having more children as a solution to what is amounting to a "caregiving crisis" in developed countries. I am simply pointing out the irony of our present situation in which prolonged life expectancy has led to its own set of challenges, including heightened expectations for children to fill the caregiving void.

It should be clear by now that Medicare has its limits in filling the need for rehabilitative therapies and skilled nursing. We all count on being the lucky ones that will not need any more than our health care insurance can provide. The old saying, "Hope for the best, but plan for the worst," best describes my position on these matters. And clearly it is not just the financing of one's care that is at issue. The choices surrounding delivery of continuing care also come into the mix for those approaching old age with their eyes open. As I have attempted to demonstrate, however, our elders have their own take on the matter. The decisions made by our parents are not always consistent with our advice or that of the experts. Thus, preexisting decisions often guide the choices that are left open to responsible family members and restrict the current options.

PRIVATE INSURANCE OR MEDICAID

There are different options today for insurance and some cover part of the costs, and so, it is always advisable to discuss alternatives with a qualified advisor, whatever your age or financial circumstances. It is also advisable to purchase insurance sooner, rather than later, with AARP advising age fifty-five for couples and between sixty and sixty-five for individuals. There are also health savings accounts and long-term care policies that are part life insurance or annuity and part long-term care to be considered. When considering long-term care insurance, questions arise, such as, should high-net-worth individuals self-insure for long-term care expenses rather than purchase insurance, and how little net worth would make it inadvisable for me to purchase insurance (since I always have the option of transferring assets and/or spending down for Medicaid)? Spending down excess income on medical bills and expenses is a way of deducting certain expenses in order to meet the Medicaid income limit in accordance to state specific rules.

If considering the Medicaid route for residential skilled nursing, it is important to know that extended care facilities can give priority to private pay applicants. Thus, being able to come up with enough money to pay privately for one year can make a difference in available options. Nursing home costs vary depending upon location and other amenities but figure on at least $100 to $150,000 annually. Hourly home health aide services range from approximately $20 to $25 per hour, in case you are considering paying out of pocket.

There are different legal mechanisms available for the protection of income and assets in meeting Medicaid eligibility requirements. For example, a pooled income trust established and managed by a charitable organization can serve as a vehicle for the protection of assets for the benefit of the Medicaid applicant. Private annuities, raising the community spouse resource allowance and gifting strategies are steps a Medicaid applicant can take to preserve their assets. Transferring assets through gifting or establishing irrevocable trusts are specific strategies. However, there are look-back periods (generally five years) during which all financial transactions made by the applicant are reviewed. Financial gifts and transfers made within the look-back period can result in a period of time during which the person who transferred the assets will be ineligible for Medicaid. States vary in policy, and therefore, it is important to know the rules in the state in which application is made. I have included reference material in the Appendix that relates to these issues. This discussion is not meant to be an exposition on the financial and legal aspects of government and private funding for long-term care. These aspects are best evaluated by an elder attorney or Medicaid expert. I would suggest with confidence that, if you are lucky enough as a designated informal caregiver to have the opportunity to guide the actions of your elders (as well as yourself), it goes without saying it is a good idea to plan. I would not venture to offer advice in this very complex area, but I can give you some examples of failure to plan, which might encourage proactivity.

MEDICAID PITFALLS

How many people have taken checks from their relatives to pay for their expenses while they were providing care? This honest use of funds for the prospective Medicaid applicant was viewed as a gift to the caregiver, who had not thought to keep receipts for all purchases and, therefore, couldn't prove that the money was spent on her loved one's needs. Gilda had to pay back a considerable amount of money that she had spent on her uncle while he was in her care. The bulk of his money had been spent down already on nursing home costs.

In another example, Barbara's father always purchased a car for her. The car represented a pattern of gift giving and, therefore, should have been viewed as a routine expense of her father's, not an attempt to reduce his assets for Medicaid eligibility. Although (at the time) this type of gift was allowed, state Medicaid refused that justification, and in the interest of not prolonging the application process, the lawyer recommended that Barbara just yield to the current requirement to return the money, which she did.

In other instances, a lot of people report resistance to seeking transfer of assets for parents or themselves because "it's welfare." If that is your attitude, then you should have no objection to having to supplement your parents' needs once their assets are exhausted. And in situations where money is not likely to run out, and one would rather pay one's own way than accept governmental assistance, you won't get any argument from me about the choice not to take advantage of Medicaid eligibility rules. Dealing with the government bureaucracy may just not be worth it to you. As I already mentioned, there was no look-back in New York until recently for community

Medicaid; therefore, transfers could be made today and application for Medicaid could be made tomorrow, but those days are over, even in New York. With careful planning, however, one's assets can be transferred, and once having met eligibility requirements, one can seamlessly qualify for government financing and better ensure uninterrupted community care or residential care, at least at the present time.

Dominica had few assets and therefore no issue of conscience. She was grateful for the aides that came to her home and accompanied her to doctors' appointments. Where there are, what might be considered, considerable assets, there may be reasons for protecting those that transcend your own self-interest. For example, Kate spent down a great deal of money on home care that might have been protected in a special needs trust for a dependent child. There are ethical questions that arise in the process of paying for care or seeking eligibility for government support for long-term care. Linda, a resident of Florida, refused to pay for her husband's care in a nursing home, stating that the amount she was allowed to keep wasn't enough to sustain her needs. Under state Medicaid rules, once the requirements of the Medicaid application were met, the state Medicaid program couldn't refuse him care. Again, don't proceed without an attorney because the Department of Social Services (DSS) may seek to recover the cost of care.

Most people who need long-term care eventually will qualify for government assistance but only after they have virtually become impoverished. The best defense is to be prepared to transfer assets well ahead of the need for care or spend down strategically.

Some people have the advantage or the financial means to readily meet the cost of care and can afford full-time home care or residential care in an extended care facility. It goes without saying that having the money is a distinct advantage. The private pay category includes private insurance, which further illustrates the benefit of planning ahead. Many people rely on a hybrid payment arrangement, which may include private payments to supplement Veterans' or Medicaid benefits. Obtaining approval for full-time home health is increasingly difficult under Medicaid, for example, which should serve as a wake-up call for people expecting to rely on government funding. Then tack on the increasing shortages in home health aides and nurses, and you have the ingredients of a perfect caregiving storm. The Veterans Aid and Attendance Pensions Benefit offers cash benefits for veterans and surviving spouses. This is a great boon to veterans (who meet service and income requirements) seeking assisted living because Medicare or Medicaid do not pay for assisted living. There is a three-year look-back period that may impact one's eligibility. Nothing is easy. Short stays in skilled nursing facilities and hospice care are covered by Medicare, but there are strict eligibility requirements.

For those with financial means, the options for securing assistance are greater for obvious reasons. As already discussed, a small percentage of older adults choose to go to life care communities, but the bulk of older adults remain in the community with home care. Home care does free the designated caregiver from much of the direct care responsibility but, as I have attempted to show, generally, does not liberate family from needing to remain intensively involved. Some private arrangements are made with live-in caregivers who dedicate their existences to the one under their care. Polly's mother Selma had live-in assistance from a woman who became a member of the family for all intents and purposes and who barely took a day off. This arrangement was not unique. Roberta's caregiver lived with her and even brought his family to stay in her home. Tina lived in her grandmother's home along with Geraldine, her grandmother's full-time aide. The cost of this care is extremely high unless one qualifies for Medicaid. In these cases, the aides were privately recruited and employed. They received higher wages than agency-employed aides. The families became very dependent on these aides with favorable outcomes, but you can see the risk in not having an agency for backup. I have also seen, as in the case of Benjamin, who eventually qualified for Medicaid, how aides secured through Medicaid have demonstrated equal loyalty. There is no one answer other than to say that it is easier to get help if you can show them the money!

THE UNKNOWN

It should be pretty obvious by now that there are more questions than easy answers. I purchased long-term care insurance at age fifty-five and have excellent coverage that would sustain my needs, no matter how extensive, for at least five years. That would give me time under present Medicaid law to protect my assets if so desired or just decide to spend down my assets to meet my personal needs. Every individual faces a different set of circumstances regarding the status of dependents, for example. My only advice is to find out what is available right now and then decide whether the security of having benefits, which you might not use, is worth the cost. I like being insured. It makes me feel more secure, sleep better at night. Other people prefer to self-insure or are prepared to navigate the labyrinth of government programs designed to avert disaster, disaster relief being the current modus operandi of long-term care delivery in the United States.

The unknown has to do with how we are going to keep up with the growing demand. Oh, yes, there are policy proposals galore regarding how to best manage our escalating health and human service costs. Choice is another operating principle of the American system, until the choices have been exhausted. In the meantime, a few words to the wise:

1. Include continuity of care planning as part of your financial planning.

2. Check out different private insurance plans if you have any assets to protect.

3. For goodness' sake, look into Veterans Benefits. Many go unclaimed!

4. Talk with your very elderly parents or grandparents about ways to protect their assets. Likelihood is they don't have private insurance.

5. *Talk with an elder attorney or a Medicaid expert.* I recently discovered that some states offer reduced penalties on transfers of assets that were made within the five-year look-back period. There are so many subtleties that only an elder attorney/Medicaid expert would have the requisite knowledge to understand and explain.

6. *Transfers or gifts have tax implications that also need to be considered. Discuss with an elder attorney or a certified public accountant.*

7. Check out the Appendix for various financial and legal resources.

CHAPTER 8

Going Off the Rails of the Crazy Train, or How to Manage Mental Challenges

At some point or another, it is not unusual to confront mental challenges in caregiving. These challenges generally increase with age associated decline in mental status or, of course, with increasing confusion associated with progressive dementia. It is not unusual for mental problems to be conflated or just confused in diagnosing mental health issues. Therefore, it is incumbent upon the caregiver to ensure proper diagnosis.

So what are these often confused mental states? In my early years in gerontology, I ran workshops that focused on distinguishing among dementia, delirium and depression as root causes of many of the same symptoms. In brief, dementia, e.g., Alzheimer's disease, is irreversible. Delirium, which is associated with many factors including, infection, metabolic imbalances, sensory deprivation, medical conditions such as stroke or heart attack, alcohol or drug intoxication, anesthesia, trauma and other factors, is reversible. The symptoms can be the same for both conditions. To confuse matters further, people who are depressed can also exhibit problems with cognition and judgment. There are clinical signs that distinguish among these conditions, for example, depressed people don't try to conceal their deficits, while early-stage dementia patients may try to hide their cognitive limitations. But to the inexperienced eye, a seriously depressed person can easily be misdiagnosed as having dementia. To complicate the situation even further, personality and psychiatric conditions, perhaps, long standing, can *further* complicate diagnostic accuracy.

According to a study conducted in 2021 by the American Geriatrics Society (AGS), between 65 percent and 90 percent of nursing home residents have a mental or behavioral problem suggesting that difficulties in managing a loved one at home may compound over time, sometimes resulting in the need for nursing home care. Although age is not associated with increased risk of mental illness in general, it is clearly a risk factor for depression and may be associated with prodromal symptoms of Alzheimer's dementia. Therefore, if most people are remaining in the community for the duration of their lives, the likelihood is that caregiving becomes more challenging from a psychiatric perspective as the loved one under your care continues to age.

CASE EXAMPLES

Recall the situation of Benjamin who went on a hunger strike as an example of strategic passive resistance. He wanted to go home from the nursing home and used every mechanism available. Of course, there was no consideration to the practicality, but eventually he accomplished his mission and returned home to a "safe" situation. Only thing was, the first aides that were assigned weren't to his liking, and usually his rejection had something to do with the appearance of the aide. He insisted upon someone young and especially "thin." His niece tried to reason with him and encountered his wrath for being "controlling." Frustration grew along with the line of aides, who, for some reason, the agency patiently kept sending for his consideration. Finally, he did settle on the two women who have been with him for years. It is critical to add that they found it in their hearts to overlook some of his personality quirks. His niece reports that she really was losing patience with his contentious behavior, but since the agency went along with his whims, she was spared the nightmare of having them refuse service. She tried reasoning but maintained respect for his "seniority." God bless her! She showed the same fortitude and tolerance that so many caregivers demonstrate in their treatment of someone who is becoming increasingly demanding and difficult to love.

Sometimes, however, particularly where the care recipient suffers from dementia and/or personality issues, the solution is not as readily fixed—if you can call the previous example as readily resolved after six months. Dementia and other behavioral conditions can foster sexual inappropriateness and hostile outbursts. It is not only hard to see your loved one behaving inappropriately in regard to acts of sexual expression, but it can be scary. Frankly, if the situation becomes too unwieldy or abusive, it is time for the caregiver to set limits. Sometimes medication can help, and sometimes other interventions may mitigate disinhibited behavior. Conversely, some medications are linked with sexual disinhibition. Distraction, such as provision of social activity, sometimes is effective, as is talking therapy, for those who still have the capacity to explore the intentions behind the behavior. But it can become too much for an individual caregiver, and often the targets of the offense are ashamed to even discuss how the behavior is impacting them personally. One caregiving wife did not want to admit how her previously high functioning husband's behavior had degenerated to the point that he assaulted her. The only advice in those situations, as in any abusive situation, is to remove yourself from danger if no other intervention proves effective.

But not all "bad" behavior reaches a point of no return. Gail reported her mother's pattern of throwing out the aides when she would get angry. Her mother, Patricia, aged eighty-seven, who suffered from a bipolar condition and also moderate-stage dementia, also threw her out on a pretty regular basis amidst hostile accusations. Gail and the aides were able to come up with a plan that would involve leaving the room where Patricia resided and just isolate themselves for a little while, giving Patricia a chance to reorient herself. Patricia was not known to hold a grudge. Nine out of ten times this strategy worked, but one time Patricia would not stop berating the aide and would not let up until she left the apartment. The aide contacted Gail, and they came up with Plan B to distract Patricia. The aide, who just went outside the door to make the call, returned with a story about how there was an incident at the railroad station and that the trains weren't running and she was frightened for her life. Now, Patricia, despite her capacity to attack, also had a capacity for deep empathy and immediately embraced the aide, who, reportedly breathed a sigh of relief, glad for the momentary reprieve.

Yes, distraction can help in some situations. Yes, sometimes even asking a person his or her fears can mitigate extreme behavior. And sometimes talk and attempts to empathize don't work.

The formal and informal caregivers may find themselves on a roller coaster ride with the one in their charge and subject to all kinds of unexpected outbursts.

It is not unusual for extreme behavior to be associated with agitation. So remove the source of the agitation, and maybe that will work to calm the fears and confusion beneath the rage. Only figuring out the source of the agitation is not that easy. Victoria was able to get through to her mother, who also exhibited very hostile behavior while residing at home, only after her mother was placed in a rehab unit following a hospitalization. It appeared to Victoria that her mother felt safer in the institution than she had felt at home. This is one example of how a residential setting can be the best option for continuing care for the loved one whom you worked so hard to keep out of a nursing home! Go figure!

Terrence, a WWII veteran, suffering from advancing dementia, would leave his home with a flashlight in the wee hours of the morning to scout around for enemies. His wife would wake up with a start, on a fairly consistent basis, and discover him "missing." She would find him looking for mines and pulling weeds in the garden in his bathrobe and gently escort him back home. Terrence had matured into being a very gentle soul, and aside from the fact that at ninety-two he would not get his hair cut, he was very compliant. His wife adored him and took care of him until the end, patiently putting up with his very fashionable pony tail.

Similarly, Jerry developed a fixation on bugs and believed that he had them on his body. There is a formal name for this, delusional parasitosis. The medication helped him somewhat, but the delusion remained with him. He was otherwise lucid most of the time. When his son asked him what he would say if somebody told him that he had bugs crawling on him, otherwise invisible to anyone else, Jerry laughed and replied, "I'd say cuckoo!" Father and son enjoyed a chuckle together and went back to picking off bugs.

If you can't beat them, sometimes there's no harm in joining them.

Imaginary friends and enemies are not unfamiliar to caregivers of loved ones with hallucinations. Naomi asked her mother if she was afraid of the person in the room that no one could see, and her mother confirmed her fear. Renee, her mother, told her that she might not see her because she "hides." Naomi decided to give a talk to the hidden "mean lady" in the room and told her to get out, in some ways entering into her mother's pathology. Renee seemed to appreciate this and later that same visit when asked if the "mean lady" had returned, Naomi said, "Who?" Apparently, she had not only received validation, but at least momentary relief from her fears.

ADVICE FOR CAREGIVERS

I have read numerous testimonials from experts about how to best cope with oppositional behavior from the one in your care, primarily a parent. I think some of the advice is a bit simplistic, to say the least. Although advice to stay calm and to soothe the savage beast with empathy and compassion sounds great, I have often found myself unable to retain an objective, rational approach with my own family members. Someone whom I respect recently said the equivalent of "Different strokes for different folks" regarding "best practices" in dealing with emotional and mental disturbances in caregiving experience. Sometimes reason and understanding just don't prevail, and sometimes "laying down the law" can achieve at least a temporary ceasefire. Sometimes not!

Bernice would often resort to calling the police when filled with dread, generally associated with imagined persecution by an aide. I discovered that this practice of calling the police is not uncommon even among residents in nursing homes. Great minds think alike! However, it takes some practice for aides and designated informal caregivers to become savvy enough to take this behavior with a grain of salt. It can be very distressful to have the police knock at your door as one can easily imagine. I have found EMS and police to be very understanding in situations that caregivers, especially designated informal caregivers, find appalling and embarrassing. I am reminded of Blanche DuBois' last line in *A Streetcar Named Desire*, "I've always depended upon the kindness of strangers," in my admiration of the ability for emergency medical, fire and police personnel to allay the tension and restore harmony with typical compassion and dispassion.

Of course, it helps to remember that the unconscionable behavior of your unlovable loved one is "nothing personal." On the other hand, we always take liberties with those with whom we are closest, and also, family history and well-entrenched interpersonal patterns of behavior can create sometimes unbearable emotional challenges for family caregivers, especially the designated informal caregiver. Hard to remain completely unscathed by emotional onslaughts. It is important to remember that the likelihood is that your unlovable (at the moment) one is probably reeling as well from the turmoil. I look at these experiences as opportunities for emotional growth. It's never too late for people to come to new understandings and to let go of enduring hurts. I would not advise anyone to count on the vulnerable individual under your care to take the initiative to modify his or her attitudes or behavior. I would not recommend that the DIC try to grin and bear the pain, either. Sometimes more impersonal assistance is more agreeable to both parties, allowing time for distancing and reappreciation.

Suffice it to say, there is often no answer to emotional challenges brought on by deteriorating behavioral factors. Caregivers who can adapt and withdraw at appropriate times and reengage at more propitious moments are not only more capable of managing the tumult, but also may find themselves more pleased with themselves to the bargain. But all of this takes a toll.

THE ART OF SURVIVING

There are many ways in which different caregivers cope with the stresses of their situation. Caregiver support groups represent a good option for some. Other caregivers are able to strike a balance between the need to self-protect and the demand to provide care. They have the motivation and the financial means to carve out some personal time while not compromising the quality of care. In some cases, such as that of Alice, caregiving demands reach the extent of being overwhelming with seemingly little chance of relief. Her husband had become increasingly dependent and, simultaneously, moodier and more stubborn. Could Alice arrange for more formal assistance? I might argue that there's always a way of securing some support, but personal choices need to be respected, and some people would just rather not engage outsiders and prefer to manage the care personally. Sometimes people just don't know that help is available, or perhaps they feel that accepting help is copping out on their responsibility for their loved ones.

Women generally provide the direct care as caregiving is still viewed as part of the woman's role. Men may even be stigmatized for providing care. According to Shannon Martin (2019) in the Easy Living Home Care blog, an estimated 66 percent of caregivers are women and they spend as much as 50 percent more time providing care than their male counterparts. In addition, women who are family caregivers are 2.5 times more likely than non-caregivers to live in poverty. On the other hand, some 20 percent of all female workers in the United States are family caregivers, and interestingly, women who work seem to be viewed with less stigma than those who devote their lives to the task. Caregiving women are more likely to suffer depression or anxiety and are less likely to participate in preventative healthcare than non-caregiving women. It is clear that emotional and physical burdens on women are excessive. Is it any wonder that the risk of going off the rails does not only accrue to the one under care, but to the care provider as well?

So to what do I attribute the art of surviving? I mentioned caregiver support groups. That's a good place to start. The popularity of utilizing Zoom and other remote options for delivering service is on the rise and has great potential in helping to ease the isolation of caregivers. Also, I would not underestimate the benefits of counseling to help manage the different facets of caregiving. I am a firm believer in the adage of "not going it alone!" Sometimes the best advice is no advice. Having a friend to validate your challenges can be enough. Alice would endorse that practice, as her friendships have been a source of great reassurance and connection.

Sometimes laughter is the best medicine. Just when you think you are at the limit of your tolerance, the one under your care will do something to remind you of why you have struggled so hard to manage his or her needs. Alice's husband would periodically tell her she's his queen while maintaining a constant stream of service requests, or Leslie would overhear Celia, her mother, telling the visiting nurse that she "tortures her daughter" indicating that there is some method to her mother's madness and that she probably wanted Leslie to feel what she was feeling in order to reduce her own sense of isolation. The nurse told Celia not to do that, and she said she wouldn't at least "for a while." After all, misery loves miserable company. Being able to smile at the craziness is always an advantage, but not everyone has that capacity. It is often best to seek out some good friends with whom to talk and get some help from wherever you can.

I also recommend establishing some kind of a routine wherever possible to create some structure and minimize the daily uncertainties. Strategic planning works for me even though I have found that my long-range planning is a moveable feast. Ask yourself, "What little step can I take to ease some of the burden today and perhaps for tomorrow?"

During these musings, nary a caregiver will fail to wonder about her or his own future caregiving requirements. We are living in an era of unprecedented aging. The average female caregiver is forty-nine years old, although with increasing longevity we can expect continuing growth in demand on women in their sixties and seventies to serve as caregivers. At the other extreme, young, primarily minority, women are already filling a principal caregiving role in society. Caregiving is a cultural phenomenon. It is also a societal conundrum.

The following chapter focuses on the inevitable question of, "Who is going to take care of me?" Or rather, "Just when I thought I might get out of deep water, here comes the next wave!"

CHAPTER 9

Who Is Going to Take Care of Me?

It's only human to wonder about what the future may hold, particularly when you have seen more than a glimpse of real-time human aging. The literature is replete with projections worthy of Nostradamus. Actually, we are already experiencing some of the predicted results of the inverted age pyramid in which aging populations are increasing and the number of children per woman is declining. We are also seeing technological advances that are making it easier for people to remain in the community. Monitoring systems, such as cameras and mobile alerts, provide additional security for people living alone. Artificial intelligence is on the rise. Technology is increasingly guiding decisions about elder care by remotely tracking daily activity of older people to free up caregivers from worry. Through developments in artificial intelligence, it has become possible to track, for example, the number of bathroom visits as a possible indication of urinary tract infection or whether your father is sleeping more than usual. These new developments represent advances over traditional life alert pendants and "nanny cams." They are touted as providing more freedom for care recipient and caregiver alike—if you consider staying up late at night to monitor your mother's movements on camera some kind of a reprieve. Yes, technology can provide greater security and perhaps greater peace of mind but may also create more social isolation for the care recipient. Robots may be effective in providing social engagement through games and are expected to be utilized to provide various kinds of assistance with activities of daily living and cognitive support. I haven't seen much of this in my experience and am not sure what to think, but this sounds like something that only the wealthier among us will be able to afford, perhaps suggestive of a "caregiving" chasm between rich and poor.

Right now, I am more impressed with the reality of the current situation in which caregiving seemingly is becoming the national pastime, maybe international pastime. Younger cohorts, particularly minority women, are providing an increasing amount of care to family members who are challenged by illness, disability and/or old age, while older people, mostly women, increasingly are providing care into their sixties and seventies. We rely on immigrant support, and yet we restrict undocumented residents from working. That's another discussion for another day. Generally, I have not witnessed any vast transformation in the way in which we manage the caregiving needs of our elderly. Relatively fewer white people than people of color reside in nursing homes, and those that do are older and stay for shorter periods of time. This is probably because white people are better able to afford resources that promote community care or enter life care communities and only resort to free-standing nursing home residence toward the end of life when advancing needs preclude community-based care.

Younger cohorts are not as wedded to the concept of marriage as were previous generations. According to Elaina William, staff writer for Famuan, only 44 percent of millennials between the ages of twenty-three and thirty-eight were married in 2019, and when it comes to marriage, "Gen Z more likely to say, 'I don't.'" Children, particularly daughters, have been the one constant care provision. What will fewer marriages, therefore fewer wives and likely fewer daughters, due to accelerating declines in birth rate, mean to the future of caregiving? Does this greater emphasis on independence also cast some doubt on the likelihood of relying on women as a sustainable caregiving resource?

The implication of all this is that we are seeing increasing need for elderly care while also experiencing transformation in expectations of younger age cohorts with regard to marriage, what makes a family and emphasis on individual fulfillment.

I don't think that younger people are necessarily less interdependent than their forebears, but certainly they have grown up in a socially distant environment, compliments of social media as well as the pandemic. They will likely be more comfortable with technological solutions and more willing to accept constraints on direct interpersonal contact. For now, throughout the age spectrum, the demands of caregiving increasingly circumscribe people's lives. This is particularly true for those without the financial resources to supplement care through "paid' or remote assistance. I don't think that is likely to change.

Medicaid will cover the total ride in a nursing home for people with little or no means. It is increasingly difficult to rely on government sources of funding to pay for round-the-clock care at home, which clearly restricts choices for those without enough supplementary informal assistance. On the positive side, board and care homes, and smaller skilled nursing homes, may provide some alternative to institutional life for our growing elderly population. For those with means, long-term care insurance comes at a hefty price that becomes even heftier if you don't enroll at a fairly young age. Planning is essential.

We are a very free country that thrives on personal choice. The only thing is that, if you don't plan and resources are limited, you either have to fill gaps in personal care through informal means or basically accept whatever the government can provide. It is not clear to me whether future generations of caregivers are going to be willing to make the sacrifices that I have witnessed in those represented in this narrative. The future of caregiving will have much to do with changes in family structure and transforming value preferences.

Will your millennial child say to you what has been expressed to me by my nearest and dearest? "Don't worry; I will find you a very nice nursing home." I responded by reassuring my prospective caregiver that I have insurance and will make my own plans and at this point they don't include a nursing home. The response was thoughtful and considerate and revealing: "I wouldn't want you to be alone. You would be lonely at home." Maybe so, and maybe not! I appreciated the sentiment and understood completely that we mutually and implicitly agreed that we would each have our separate lives and solutions. Many older people of my generation have moved closer to their children as they have aged. That makes complete sense. Many will benefit from this proximity as their needs increase. Many also are investigating life care communities because they do not want to become a burden to their children, and with life expectancy having reached centenarian status for some (not all) cohorts, longevity is part of the mix in planning. Most of the people I know have at least expressed the idea that they want to retain their independence from their children, whereas these same people have also been expected and have expected themselves to provide the lion's share of care for their parents and spouses. Expectations are changing, and expectations also change with increased engagement with the practical realities of the situation.

There is no easy answer to the question of, "Who will take care of me?" My advice is just to focus on the here and now and do what you can to prepare for your own continuing care, in the same way that you might have planned for your retirement or your children's passage to adulthood. It is important to remember that we all learn from our experience, particularly our mistakes.

The following Afterword offers some takeaways that I have garnered from my journey through the caregiving maze and some reflections on the courageous individuals whom I have had the privilege of meeting along this path of meaning.

AFTERWORD

CAREGIVING CONFIDENTIAL

The research and writing of this narrative have inspired my own personal interest in helping others get through the trials, tribulations and triumphs of giving and also receiving care. The caregivers that I have encountered have contributed deeply to my understanding of the dynamics of caregiving, the role of the caregiver and the path to the meaning that caregiving represents.

PROFILE OF THE CAREGIVER

In spite of all the differences among the designated informal caregivers characterized in this book, certain patterns emerge. It goes without saying that these people, mostly women, are courageous and, in many ways, selfless individuals who have put the caregiving needs of their loved ones ahead of their own. I am reminded of Arlene who neglected her own health in caring for her husband and who needed emergency bypass surgery from which, happily, she recovered. In later years, her daughter, Jill, reciprocated the care her mother gave to her father by fulfilling the role of a designated informal caregiver for Arlene. The apple doesn't fall far from the tree! Arlene did not face as arduous a caregiving task with her own mother and father because they died before they had become as compromised as she would become. There is a downside to longevity, even though some people remain fairly independent well into very advanced age. Most of the caregivers interviewed were raised with a sense of familial responsibility and did not resent or regret providing care. One caregiver put it beautifully in saying that, despite the drain on her own personal resources, including her health, she would do it all over again for the opportunity to have her mother back in her life. It's possible that hindsight does not offer the most objective perspective, but nevertheless, people seem to choose to remember their loved ones in the best possible light. Another caregiver said that it's best to overlook a lot of your parents' behavior during the final stage of life or at least not to let it alter your memories of easier times.

I have made it pretty clear that I have served multiple times in the role of a designated informal caregiver. I am humbled by the extraordinary efforts made by children, spouses, professionals, home health aides and neighbors who have been generous in the support of my family members. A beloved doctor reminded me of the afore-mentioned maxim, "It takes a village." It might not be an original thought, but it works. I think those caregivers who could embrace available support from others willing to lend a hand benefited from the bonding experience as well as any proffered help.

There seems to be a design to the caregiving experience in which requirements generally compound over time, giving the care-giver, as well as the recipient of care, time to adjust. Those caregivers who were able to go with the flow and make adjustments along the uncertain path seemed to be able to find a more or less comfort-able stride.

Of course, humor always helps, and humor requires interaction with somebody else. I think it's the interaction that is the critical ingredient. Many of us have been raised according to the adage, "When you smile, the world smiles with you, and when you cry, you cry alone." Being able to cry as well as laugh with a trusted friend can be counted on to help relieve the tension and strife. Thus, even Paul, the bass fisherman mentioned in an early chapter, who generally preferred his solitude, joined and acknowledged the merit of a caregiving support group.

Sometimes the challenges become so great that caregiver burnout occurs. It's hard to admit defeat. Sometimes a break from the duties is sufficient, and sometimes the burnout is a signal that the time has come for an adjustment in the care.

I personally have confronted this with both my parents. Each of them transitioned at a very advanced age to a nursing home because their needs surpassed our ability to provide care at home. Both made the transition after many years of community-based caregiving. Better planning might have avoided this outcome, but they were not receptive to my professional suggestions, and I simply accommodated their requests, at least for a long period of time. I have learned a few things from this experience.

WHAT I HAVE LEARNED

1. There is no script. There are only choices to be made at successive intervals.

2. Caregiving can be onerous.

3. Getting angry is ok, but it's better to get help figuring things out.

4. I have repeatedly said, and I will once more: get started on a plan (if you haven't already) for financing this venture and also evaluating options for care.

5. Consult with an elder lawyer, not just your financial planner or accountant or your general attorney, for that matter. Continuity of care issues impact financial and estate planning and vice versa.

6. My most important lesson relates to how caregiving has made me a different (albeit slightly) person and professional.

THE ALMOST NEW ME

I have to take you back to my dad, my first personal caregiving subject, who wanted to be reassured that he could go home. I made the mistake of thinking that I could get him to be rational about planning. I was very committed to planning. I have always been very strategic in my planning. It didn't work. All he wanted to hear from me was that he could aspire to go home. I visited him consistently and consistently tried to reason. I should have reassured him. Now you might say that I would have been holding out false hope. Well, so what? What harm would reassuring him have done? I am not so sure anymore. Fast forward to the present and after years of providing care for my mother, I am less likely to tell her that her fate is sealed even though it's pretty obvious to everyone who knows her that she is more content right now at the tender age of "going on 101," having all of her needs met efficiently and, from all accounts, compassionately by professionals in a skilled nursing facility.

Ever since our experience with my dad, my sibling and I have been opposed to nursing home placement. And fortunately, my mother was able to remain home at the peak of the pandemic and now is fully vaccinated in a Covid-free environment.

But when Mother asks about leaving, even though her home has become anathema to her, I tell her we are going out and about in Manhattan as soon as the weather improves. Now that she's living in Manhattan, we can go back to enjoying the city and she is spared the suburbs, which, as a Brooklyn girl, she never really liked. I think you get the gist of this. Mother actually responded favorably to these comments. At least for the moment. Tomorrow is another day.

So, in conclusion, let me just say, *thank you*, for taking your time to wade through these pages, and if you are currently a caregiver, take pride and prepare for an unfolding situation. I have learned to live with ambiguity and give up the need to complete the picture while managing the inevitable twists and turns, not always with equanimity. The one thing that hasn't changed, and which has been my salvation, has been my ability to laugh at myself and with others.

CARE-YE ON!

APPENDIX

TOPIC REFERENCES

THE HEALTH AND LONG-TERM CARE SYSTEMS

Health Care and Insurance Industries Mobilize to Kill "Medicare for All"

https://www.nytimes.com/2019/02/23/us/politics.medicare-for-all-lobbyists.html

Older People Need Geriatricians. Where Will They Come From?

https://www.nytimes.com/2020/01/03/health/geriatricians-shortage.html?smid=em-share

"The System is So Broken": What It's Like in Long-Term Care Right Now?

https://www.chatelaine.com/living/long-term-care-canada/

How Referrals Work with Your Health Insurance

https://www.verywellhealth.com/what-is-a-referral-health-insurance-1738605

The Specialist Referral: Do Primary Care Providers Have All the Information They Need? 3M Inside Angle

https://insideangle.3m.com/his/blog-post/
specialist-referral-primary-care-providers-information-need/

The Lawyers and Doctors Making America's Crisis Worse

https://www.theatlantic.com/ideas/archive/2021/01/
lawyers-and-doctors-making-americas-crisis-worse/617673/

For the Insurance Lobby, Old Habits Are Hard to Break: Center for American Progress

https://www.americanprogress.org/article/
for-the-insurance-lobby-old-habits-are-hard-to-break/

NYTimes.com: Older People Need Geriatricians. Where Will They Come From?

https://www.nytimes.com/2020/01/03/health/geriatricians-short-
age.html?smid=em-share

"Patient Struggles in Navigating Healthcare"

https://www.managedhealthcareexecutive.com/view/
patient-struggles-navigating-healthcare

NYTimes: Tallying the Cost of Growing Older

https://nyti.ms/3mmr9xp

"Government Assistance and Funding for Caregivers in Canada, Elizz"

https://elizz.com/planning/
government-assistance-and-funding-for-caregivers-in-canada/

Care for America's Elderly and Disabled People Relies on Immigrant Labor/Health Affairs

https://www.healthaffairs.org/doi/10.1377/hlthaff.2018.05514

Comparing Long-Term Care in Canada and United States, Elder Guru

https://www.elderguru.com/
comparing-long-term-care-in-canada-and-the-united-states/

What You Need to Know About the Change to the Stark Law

https://www.digrad.com/stark-law-changes-2021/

DEMOGRAPHICS OF CAREGIVERS AND AGING POPULATIONS:

Ethnic Differences in Caregiving: Adult Daughters and Elderly Mothers, Terry Tirrito, Ilene Nathanson, 1994

https://journals.sagepub.com/doi/
abs/10.1177/088610999400900106

Women and Caregiving: Why Daughters Are Still the #1 Caregiver

https://easylivingfl.com/blog/women-and-caregiving

Women and Caregiving: Facts and Figures, Family Caregiver Alliance

https://www.caregiver.org/resource/women-and-caregiving-facts-
and -figures/

Demographics of Aging Populations: Providing Healthy and Safe Foods as We Age, NCBI Bookshelf

https://www.ncbi.nlm.nih.gov/books/NBK51841/

Very Old Folks at Home: Even at 95, Majority Still Live in Homes They Own

https://www.forbes.com/sites/ashleabeling/2012/08/07/from-home-
ownership-to-renting-who-is-making-the-switch/?sh=1bec-
31e82a47

"Black Americans Face Widening Life Expectancy Gap, Biggest Since 1998"

https://www.wfyi.org/news/articles/black-americans-face-widen-
ing-life-expectancy-gap-biggest-since-1998

"Caregiver Statistics: Demographics-Family Caregiver Alliance"

https://www.caregiver.org/resource/
caregiver-statistics-demographics/

Cultural Diversity and Caregiving

https://www.apa.org/pi/about/publications/caregivers/faq/cultural-diversity

Community and Culture Help Black Caregivers Cope with the Challenges of Family Caregiving

https://feeds.aarp.org/caregiving/basics/info-2021/african-american-cargivers-cope-better.html?_amp=true

"Aging While Black: The Crisis among Black Americans as They Grow Old/ NAACP"

https://naacp.org/articles/aging-while-black-crisis-among-black-americans-they-grow-old

"Caregiving for Older Family Member Pew Research Center"

https://www.pewresearch.org/social-trends/2013/01/30/caregivng-for-older-family-members/

"Millennials Face Unusual Burdens When Caring for Aging Parents"

https://www.blackenterprise.com/millennials-face-unusual-burdens-when-caring-for-aging-parents/amp/

"More and More Millennials Are Caregivers for Older Family Members, NPR"

https://www.npr.org/2019/03/16/702698968/as-parents-and-grandparents-age-more-and-more-millennials-are-family-caregivers

Comparison of Informal Caregiving by Black and White Older Adults in a Community Population, PubMed

https://pubmed.ncbi.nlm.nih.gov/11129751/

"Informal Caregiving"

https://geriatrics.stanford.edu/ethnomed/african_american/disparities/physician/caregiving.html#:~:text=In%20general%20African%20American%20caregivers,resources%20(Haley%2C%201993)

"Hispanic Millennials Are More Likely to Become Caregivers for Elder Relatives/Memory Well

https://news.memorywell.com/2019/07/10/hispanic-millennials-are-more-likely-to-become-caregivers-for-elder-relatives/

Stay Calm and Care On: 4 Millennials Share the Joys and Pains of Becoming the Family Caregiver, Vox

https://www.vox.com/ad/20937084/millennial-caregiving-caring-baby-boomer-generation

The Challenging Life of a Millennial Caregiver, Time

https://time.com/5282340/millennial-caregivers-baby-boomers/

"Culture, Caregiving, and Health: Exploring the influence of Culture on Family Caregiver Experiences"

https://www.hindawi.com/journals/isrn/2014/689826/

"Distribution of African Americans in Residential Care/Assisted Living and Nursing Homes: More Evidence of Racial Disparity?"

https://www.ncbi.nlm.nih.gov/pmc/articles/PMC1447229/

"Nursing Home Residents Percentage by Ethnicity U.S. 2014, Statista"

https://www.statista.com/statistics/717618/percent-of-nursing-home-residents-in-us-by-ethnicity/

CAREGIVING CHALLENGES

Too Often, Daughters are Family Caregivers. Better In-Home Care Options Would Change That, MS Magazine

https://www.msmagazine.com/2021/11/30/in-home:

Home Health Care Aides Are in Short Supply, NPR

https://www.npr.org/2021/09/28/1031651663/shortage-home-health-aides-elderly

"More Elderly Parents Moving In with Adult Children, News Desk"

https://www.interimhealthcare.com/about-in-terim-healthcare/news-media/news-desk/more-elderly-parents-moving-in-with-adult-children/

7 Steps to Take When Aging Parents Need Help, DailyCaring

https://dailycaring.com/7-steps-to-take-when-aging-parents-need-help/

Home Care/ComfortLife.ca "Home Care/ComfortLife.ca"

https://www.comfortlife.ca/home-care

Caregiver Well-Being and Burden: Variations by Race/Ethnicity and Care Recipient Nativity Status/Innovation in Aging, Oxford Academic

https://academic.oup.com/innovativeage/article4/6/igaa045/5905942

"Informal Caregiving"

https://geriatrics.stanford.edu/ethnomed/african_american/disparities/physician/caregiving.html#:~:text=In%20general%20African%20American%20caregivers,resources%20(Haley%2C%201993)

"The Psychology of Home: Why Where You Live Means So Much, The Atlantic"

https://amp.theatlantic.com/amp/article/249800/

"Symbolism of Home#2: The Image of our House and Our Inner Being"

https://www.briancollinson.ca/index.php.2017/09/symbolism-of-home-2-the-image-of-the-house-our-inner-being.html

"Home is Where the Heart Is, But Where is "Home"? Psychology Today

https://www.psychologytoday.com/us/blog/out-the-ooze/201508/home-is-where-the-heart-is-where-is-home?amp

SUPPORT SERVICES/RESOURCES

The Long-Term Care Benefit Many Veterans are Missing Out On

https://www.forbes.com/sites/nextavenue/2o017/11/10/
the-long-term-care-benefit-many-veterans-are-missing-out-on/

What Services Do Hospice Patients & Their Families Receive?

https://www.crossroadshospice-pal-
liative-care-blog/2019/january/23/
what-services-do-hospice-patients-their-families-receive/

"When Is the Right Time for Hospice Care?

https://www.forbes.com/sites/nextavenue/2018/08/01/
when-is-the-right-time-for-hospice-care/amp/

Naturally Occurring Retirement Community (NORC) Office for
the Aging

https://aging.ny.gov/
naturally-occurring-retirement-community-norc

NORCS: The Benefits and Drawbacks of Naturally Occurring
Retirement Communities, SeniorsMatter

https://www.seniorsmatter.com/norcs-the-benefits-and-draw-
backs-of-naturally-occurring-retirement-communities/2492384/

ArchCare CEO: This is the Moment for PACE – Skilled
Nursing News

https://skillednursingnews.com/2021/07/
archcare-ceo-this-is-the-moment-for-pace/

MENTAL HEALTH CHALLENGES

2020 Alzheimer's Disease Facts and Figures, 2020 Alzheimer's & Dementia, Wiley Online Library/#

https://alz-journals.onlinelibrary.wiley.com/doi/full/10.1002/alz.12068#:~:text=Age%20is%20the%20greatest%20of,or%20older%20have%20Alzheimer's%20dementia

Nursing Home Residents with Dementia Cannot Consent to Sexual Relationships, Illinois Nursing Home Abuse Blog

https://blog.levinperconti.com/nursing-home-residents-with-dementia-cannot-consent-to-sexual-relationships/

Mental Health in Nursing Homes/Managing Emotional Health

https://www.nursinghomeabuse.org/resources/nursing-home-mental-health/#:~:text=According%20to%20a%20study%20from,mental%20or%20behavioral%20health%20problem

Social Support is Key to Nursing Home Length of Stay Before Death

https://www.ucsf.edu/news/2010/0898172/social-support-key-nursing-home-length-stay-death#:~:text=The%20average%20length%20of%20stay,median%20stay%20of%20eight%20months

Under-65 Population with Serious Mental Illness Continues to Grow in Nursing Homes, Analysis Finds, Clinical Daily News, McKnight's Long-Term Care News

https://www.mcknights.com/news/clinical-news/serious-mental-illness-under-65-population-continue-to-grow-in-nursing-homes-analysis-finds/

Elders Who Abuse Their Family Caregivers, AgingCare.com

https://www.agingcare.com/articles/elders-abusing-their-adult-children-or-caregivers-137122.htm

RESIDENTIAL OPTIONS AND CHALLENGES

40 Need-to-Know Nursing Home Statistics

https://etcactics.com/blog/nursing-home-statistics

Must-Know Statistics about Long-Term Care, 2019
Edition, Morningstar

https://www.morningstar.com/articles/957487/
must-know-statistics-about-long-term-care-2019-edition

How'd We Get Here? The History of Nursing Homes, Next Avenue

https://www.nextavenue.org/history-of-nursing-homes/

Who Lives in Assisted Living? SeniorCare.com

https://www.seniorcare.com/assisted-living/resources/
who-lives-in-assisted-living-/

Assisted Living Statistics 2022: Population and Facilities

https://www.consumeraffairs.com/assisted-living/statistics.html

Assisted Living vs. Board and Care Homes: A Place for Mom

https://www.aplaceformom.com/caregiver-resources/articles/
assisted-living-vs-board-care-homes

Assisted Living Kicks Out the Frail 'Cause "We Can't Take Care of
You any Longer", Kaiser Health News

https://khn.org/news/assisted-living-kicks-out-the-frail-cause-we-
can't-take-care-of-you-any-longer/

Group Homes an Alternative for Seniors Who Can't Age in Place

https://feeds.aarp.org/caregiving/basics/info-2020/group-homes.
html?_amp=true

7 Reasons to Consider Assisted Living

https://www.umh.org/assisted-independent-living-blog/
bid/317889/7-Rreasons-to-Consider-Assisted-Living

Assisted Living Options for Low-Income Elders, AssistedLiving.org

https://www.assistedliving.org/
assisted-living-options-low-income-elders/

Know Your Retirement Community's Exit Options, MarketWatch

https://www.marketwatch.com/story/
retirement-communities-read-the-contract-2013-06-19

Watch Out for These Hidden Costs of Assisted Living, Care.
com Resources

https://www.care.com/c/hidden-costs-assisted-living/

FINANCIAL AND LEGAL CHALLENGES

7 Ways to Judge a Retirement Community's Financial Health

https://www.nytimes.com/2018/03/09/business/retirement-community-financial -health.html

Looming Crisis in Continuing Care Retirement Communities, Toptal

https://www.toptal.com/finance/fundraising/looming-crisis-in-continuing-care-retirement-communities-ccrc

How to Restructure Your Assets to Qualify for Medicaid / Kiplinger

https://www.kiplinger.com/personal-finance/insurancw/health-insurance/603705/how-to-restructure-your-assets-to-qualify-for

Benefit or Backfire: Navigating the Medicaid Irrevocable Trust

https://www.commonwealth.com/insights/benefit-or-backfire-navigating-the-irrevocable--medicaid-trust

Protecting Your House from Medicaid Estate Recovery

https://www.elderlawanswers.com/protecting-your-house-from-medicaid-estate-recovery-12155

Medicaid Planning That Won't Work: Asset Transfers That Incur a Medicare Penalty / Nolo

https://www..nolo.com/legal-encyclopedia/medicaid-planning-asset-transefers-incur-medicare-penalty.html

How Medicaid Spend Down Works: Rules, Exemptions & Strategies

https://www.medicaidplanningassistance.org/medicaid-spend-down/

Medicaid Pitfall: Paying for Private Aids (July 14, 2020),

Medicaid Planning Archives https://www.fendrickmorganlaw.com

How the Medicaid Look-Back Period Works

https://www.medicaidplanningassistance.org/
medicaid-look-back-period/

How Gifts Can Affect Medicaid Eligibility

https://www.elderlawanswers.com/
how-gifts-can-affect-medicaid-eligibility-10006

Spousal Impoverishment: Medicaid Spend-Down Rules for Married Couples, AgomgCare.com

https://www.agingcare.com/articles/medicaid-spend-down-for-spouses-158628.htm

"When Should Family Caregivers Apply for Medicaid for a Loved One?"

https://feeds.aarp.org/caregiving/health/info-2021/when-to-apply-for-medicaid.html?_amp=true

How Can I Pay for Nursing Home Care? Medicare

https://www.medicare.gov/what-medicare-covers/
what-part-a-covers/how-can-i-pay-for-nursing-home-care

Crisis Medicaid Planning the Promissory/Gift Loan Plan, Albany Elder Law Lawyers

https://www.burkecasserly.com/crisis-medicaid-plan-ning-the-promissory-gift-loan-plan.html

Buy Long-Term Care Insurance at the Right Age to Get the Best Value

https://feeds.aarp.org/caregiving/financial-legal/info=2019/when-to-buy-long-term-care-insurance.html?_amp=true

When Should You Consider a Pooled Trust? Special Needs Alliance

https://www.specialneedsalliance.org/blog/when-should-you-consider-a-pooled-trust/

Nursing Home Costs in 2022 by State and Type of Care

https://www.seniorliving.org/nursing-homes/costs/

Should Some Clients Self-Insure for Long-Term Care

https://www.commonwealth.com/insights/should/-some-clients-self-insure-for-long-term-care

Should I Buy Long-Term Care Insurance?

https://www.iii.org/article/should-i-buy-long-term-care-insurance

Government Assistance and Funding for Caregivers in Canada, Elizz

https://elizz.com/planning/government/-assistance-and-funding-for-caregivers-in-canada/

The Sobering Cost of Long-Term Care: A Guide to Paying for Care Without Breaking the Bank, MoneyGeek.com

FUTURE OF CAREGIVING

Will the Nursing Home of the Future be an Actual Home? POLITICO

https://www.politico.com/news/agenda/2021/04/30/nursing-home-future-483460

What Does the Future Hold for Senior Care?

https://aging.com/what-does-the-future-hold-for-senior-care/

The Future of Elder Care is Here, and It's Artificial Intelligence, US news, The Guardian

https://www.theguardian.com/us-news/2021/jun/03/elder-care-artificial-intelligence-software

Easterseals/For Caregivers: Planning for the Future

https://www.easterseals.com/explore-resources/for-caregivers/caregivers-planning-for-the-future.html

What the Future of Caregiving Looks Like

https://www.forbes.com/sites/nextavenue/2017/05/30/what-the-future-of-caregiving-looks-like/?sh=4fb35cec398f